Step by Step Dividend Investing

STEP BY STEP DIVIDEND INVESTING

The Dirty Little Secrets of Sector Dividend Investing (What Wall Street Won't Tell You)

by

John King

Introduction

Dividend investing is often portrayed as a slow-and-steady path to wealth—reliable paychecks, compounding returns, and financial freedom. But behind the success stories lie brutal realities most investors won't admit: Most dividend portfolios fail.

Why? Because too many investors chase high yields without understanding sustainability, ignore sector risks, and underestimate tax traps. They read about retirees living off dividends but don't see the ones who went broke after a single dividend cut. They hear about "set-it-and-forget-it" income streams but aren't warned about invisible fees, reinvestment hurdles, and inflation erosion.

This chapter isn't another rosy case study of a lucky investor who struck gold. Instead, we'll expose:

•The "survivorship bias" deception—why most dividend portfolios don't survive long-term.
•The real strategies of successful dividend investors (not just the ones who got lucky).
•The hidden pitfalls—from tax bombs to psychological traps —that derail even disciplined investors.

Whether you're building a retirement portfolio or seeking passive income, understanding these **hard truths** will separate you from the investors who learn them **the expensive way**. Let's dive in.

Chapter 1: Dividend Investing Basics

Dividend investing is a time-tested strategy that combines capital growth with consistent income. Whether you're just starting out or looking to diversify your portfolio, understanding the basics of dividend investing is essential for long-term financial success.

1.1 What Are Dividends?

Dividends are periodic payments made by companies to their shareholders, typically from profits. These payments serve as a reward to investors for owning stock and represent a share in the company's earnings. Dividends can be issued in various forms:

- **Cash dividends** – Direct payments made in cash.
- **Stock dividends** – Additional shares given to investors.
- **Special dividends** – One-time payments that aren't part of the regular payout schedule.

Dividends are most commonly issued by established, profitable companies, particularly in industries like utilities, consumer staples, and financials.

1.2 How Dividend Investing Works

Dividend investing involves purchasing stocks specifically for their income-producing potential. The goal is to build a portfolio that generates regular dividend payments, which can be:

- **Reinvested** to purchase more shares (compounding returns over time), or
- **Used as income** to supplement living expenses or retirement needs.

Key elements of this strategy include:

- **Dividend yield** – The percentage of a stock's price paid out annually in dividends.
- **Payout ratio** – The percentage of earnings paid out as dividends, indicating sustainability.
- **Dividend growth rate** – The rate at which a company increases its dividend.

1.3 Pros and Cons of Dividend Stocks

✅ **Pros:**

- **Regular Income**: Great for retirees or passive income seekers.
- **Lower Volatility**: Dividend-paying stocks tend to be more stable.
- **Compounding Returns**: Reinvested dividends accelerate portfolio growth.
- **Inflation Hedge**: Dividends can grow over time, preserving purchasing power.

❌ **Cons:**

- **Taxable Income**: Dividends may be taxed depending on the investor's country and account type.
- **Limited Capital Gains**: High-yield stocks may offer less price appreciation.

- **Dividend Cuts**: In tough economic times, companies may reduce or eliminate dividends.

1.4 Types of Dividend Stocks

Dividend-paying stocks are not one-size-fits-all. Here are the main categories:

- **Dividend Growth Stocks**: Companies that consistently increase their dividends (e.g., Dividend Aristocrats).
- **High Yield Stocks**: Offer high dividend payments but may carry more risk.
- **REITs**: Real estate investment trusts that are legally required to pay out most of their earnings as dividends.
- **Preferred Stocks**: A hybrid security that often pays fixed dividends and has priority over common stocks.

1.5 Getting Started with Dividends

To begin investing in dividend stocks:

1. **Choose a brokerage account** – Look for platforms that offer commission-free trading and DRIP options.
2. **Research dividend stocks or ETFs** – Use filters for yield, growth, and payout ratio.
3. **Start small and diversify** – Spread investments across sectors and regions.
4. **Reinvest or collect income** – Set up automatic reinvestment or create a withdrawal plan.

5. **Track and rebalance** – Use tools to monitor income growth and portfolio allocation.

Summary:
Dividend investing is a robust, income-generating strategy suitable for investors at any stage. By understanding how dividends work and selecting the right types of stocks, you can create a portfolio that not only grows in value but also pays you along the way.

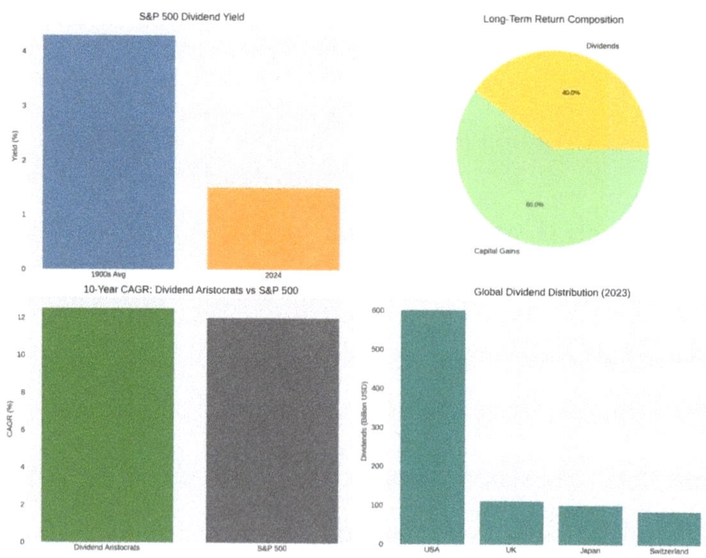

- ***S&P 500 Dividend Yield** – Shows the drop from historical averages (~4.3%) to today's yield (~1.5%).*
- ***Return Composition** – Highlights how dividends contribute around 40% to long-term total returns.*

- ***CAGR Comparison*** – *Dividend Aristocrats slightly outperform the S&P 500 over 10 years.*
- ***Global Dividend Distribution*** – *Shows which countries are the biggest sources of dividend income.*

Chapter 2: Dividend Growth Investing

Dividend Growth Investing (DGI) is a strategy focused on acquiring stocks from companies that consistently increase their dividends over time. This approach not only provides reliable income but also helps fight inflation and enhances long-term wealth creation through compounding.

2.1 Top Dividend Growth Stocks

Dividend growth stocks are typically large-cap companies with stable earnings and a track record of increasing payouts. Some of the most well-known dividend growth stocks include:

- **Johnson & Johnson (JNJ)**
- **Procter & Gamble (PG)**
- **Coca-Cola (KO)**
- **Microsoft (MSFT)**

These companies are often part of the **Dividend Aristocrats** list, which includes firms that have raised dividends for 25 consecutive years or more.

Key Characteristics:

- Strong cash flow
- Low to moderate payout ratios
- Long-term business stability
- Shareholder-friendly capital allocation

2.2 How to Analyze Dividend Growth

Before investing in a dividend growth stock, investors should evaluate:

- **Dividend Growth Rate**: A higher growth rate (5–10% annually) is ideal for long-term wealth.
- **Payout Ratio**: Indicates dividend safety. A ratio under 60% is typically considered healthy.
- **Earnings Growth**: Strong earnings support dividend increases.
- **Free Cash Flow**: Confirms that the company can afford ongoing dividend hikes.
- **Debt Levels**: Excessive debt may limit a company's ability to raise dividends.

Use tools like **Dividend Channel**, **Seeking Alpha**, or **Simply Safe Dividends** for fundamental analysis.

2.3 Benefits of Dividend Growth Investing

- **Compounding Power**: Reinvesting growing dividends accelerates wealth over time.
- **Inflation Hedge**: Increasing dividends help maintain purchasing power.
- **Downside Protection**: DGI stocks tend to be less volatile in bear markets.
- **Income Predictability**: Reliable and increasing cash flow can be used for retirement planning or financial independence.

Example: A stock growing its dividend at 7% annually will double its payout in about 10 years, thanks to the Rule of 72.

2.4 Dividend Growth Investing Strategies

There are multiple ways to build a DGI portfolio:

□ Core & Satellite

- **Core**: Blue-chip growth stocks with consistent dividend history.
- **Satellite**: Smaller or higher-growth companies with shorter histories but strong potential.

🛠 Dividend Reinvestment Plan (DRIP)

- Automatically reinvest dividends to purchase more shares and benefit from dollar-cost averaging.

Income Ladder

- Select stocks with different payout dates to ensure consistent monthly income.

Screening Criteria

- Use stock screeners to filter companies by dividend history, payout ratio, sector, and market cap.

2.5 Historical Performance of Dividend Growers

Studies have consistently shown that dividend growers outperform non-dividend payers over the long term. According to research:

- **Dividend growers** tend to offer better risk-adjusted returns.
- They show **lower volatility** during market corrections.
- **Reinvested dividends** contribute significantly to total returns.

For example, between 1973 and 2022, dividend-growing stocks delivered an annualized return that significantly outpaced the broader S&P 500 index.

Summary:
Dividend Growth Investing is a powerful, long-term strategy that balances income generation with capital appreciation. By focusing on high-quality, shareholder-friendly companies, investors can build a portfolio that not only pays today but also pays more tomorrow.

Chapter 3: High Dividend Yield Stocks

High dividend yield stocks are attractive to investors seeking immediate, substantial income. While the promise of bigger payouts is tempting, understanding the balance between yield and risk is crucial for long-term success.

3.1 Best High-Yield Stocks in 2025

As of 2025, some of the top high-yield stocks offering stable or rising dividends include:

- **Altria Group (MO)** – Tobacco giant with consistent cash flow and over 8% yield.
- **AT&T (T)** – Telecommunications firm with a strong dividend history.
- **Energy Transfer (ET)** – Midstream energy company offering yields north of 9%.
- **Lumen Technologies (LUMN)** – Telecom with an ultra-high yield (though riskier).

High-yield doesn't always mean high quality—vetting financials, industry stability, and management is essential.

3.2 Risks of High-Yield Investing

✕ Dividend Traps

Stocks may appear attractive with high yields, but a closer look might reveal:

- **Falling share prices**
- **Unsustainable payout ratios**
- **Declining revenue or earnings**

⚠ Common Risks:

- **Dividend Cuts**: The higher the yield, the more likely the company might reduce payouts during downturns.
- **Sector Volatility**: Sectors like energy, telecom, and REITs may be cyclical or heavily debt-reliant.
- **Market Mispricing**: Sometimes high yield reflects investor pessimism—not value.

Example: A stock yielding 12% might face a dividend suspension due to falling cash flow.

3.3 Screening for High-Yield Stocks

Use the following criteria when looking for strong high-yield opportunities:

- **Dividend Yield > 5%**, but not excessively high (>10% often signals distress).
- **Payout Ratio < 80%**, or ideally based on free cash flow (especially for REITs).
- **Positive EPS and Revenue Growth** over 3-5 years.
- **Debt-to-Equity < 1.5** (debt-fueled yields are risky).
- **Dividend History** of at least 5 years.

Tools: Finviz, Seeking Alpha, GuruFocus, Morningstar, and Simply Safe Dividends.

3.4 Dividend Yield vs. Company Health

High yield alone isn't enough. A healthy dividend stock shows:

Metric	Healthy Range
Dividend Yield	4–7%
Payout Ratio	< 70%
Debt/Equity	< 1.5
Free Cash Flow	Positive & Growing
Dividend Growth	Ideally increasing, even slowly

Red Flag: If yield is rising while price drops and earnings shrink—it's likely a dividend trap.

3.5 High-Yield vs. Safe Dividends

Here's how **high yield stocks** compare to **safe dividend stocks**:

Feature	High-Yield Stocks	Safe Dividend Stocks
Yield	6–10%+	2–4%
Risk	Higher	Lower

Feature	High-Yield Stocks	Safe Dividend Stocks
Sectors	REITs, energy, telecom	Consumer staples, healthcare
Growth Potential	Moderate	Higher long-term sustainability
Suitability	Income now	Income + capital preservation

Pro Tip: Blend both in a portfolio to balance income and longevity.

Summary:
High dividend yield stocks offer enticing income potential but come with increased scrutiny. Avoid chasing yield blindly—evaluate the company's fundamentals, stability, and ability to maintain payouts over time. Done right, they can powerfully enhance an income-focused investment strategy.

3.1 Best High-Yield Stocks in 2025

Company	Sector	Dividend Yield	Dividend Stability	Notes
Altria Group (MO)	Consumer Staples	~8.5%	Stable	Strong cash flow; tobacco industry
AT&T (T)	Telecom	~7.1%	Moderate	Debt-heavy; steady demand
Energy Transfer (ET)	Energy	~9.3%	Moderate	Volatile sector; high payout
Lumen Tech (LUMN)	Telecom	12%+	Weak	Potential dividend tra

🗠 Sector Risk Heatmap

Sector	Volatility Risk	Dividend Cut History
Energy	● High	● Frequent
Telecom	□ Moderate	□ Occasional
Consumer Staples	□ Low	□ Rare
REITs	□ Moderate	● During recessions

🔍 3.3 Screening Criteria Table

Metric	Ideal Range	Why It Matters
Dividend Yield	4%–7%	Attractive but usually safe
Payout Ratio	< 70%	Indicates dividend is sustainable
Debt-to-Equity	< 1.5	Keeps financial risk manageable
Earnings Growth	Positive YoY	Supports future dividends
Dividend History	≥ 5 Years	Shows commitment to shareholders

⚖ 3.4 Yield vs. Health Comparison Chart

📈 Yield vs. Dividend Safety (Visual Chart)

Yield | ⚠

| ⚠

| ⚠

| □

| □

|____________________________

Low Safety High

□ = Ideal zone

⚠ = Risk of dividend cut

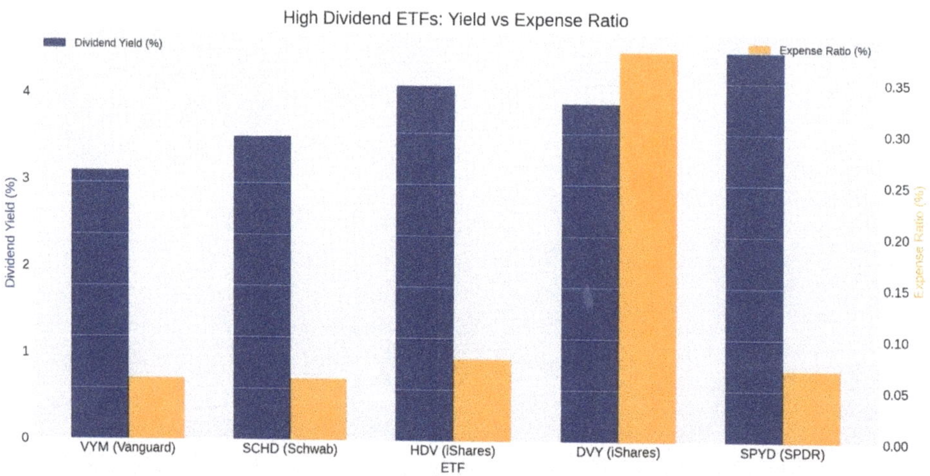

*Here's a bar chart comparing popular **high-dividend ETFs**:*

- ***Blue Bars:** Dividend yield (%)*
- ***Orange Bars:** Expense ratio (%)*

◈ ***SPYD** offers the highest yield (~4.5%)*
◈ ***SCHD** and **VYM** have low fees (0.06%) with solid yields*
◈ ***HDV** and **DVY** provide higher yields but at slightly higher costs*

Chapter 4: Dividend Aristocrats The Truth Behind the Hype

*"In 1989, investors could buy all 26 Dividend Aristocrats for 10,000.*By2024,thatportfoliowouldbeworthover*1.2 million —with dividends reinvested. But here's the catch: Half of the original Aristocrats were kicked out along the way. This chapter reveals what no one tells you about these so-called 'elite' dividend stocks."*

Dividend Aristocrats (S&P 500 companies with 25+ years of consecutive dividend increases) are often marketed as set-and-forget investments. But blindly trusting them is a costly mistake. Here's what you really need to know.

Section 1: The Dark Side of Dividend Aristocrats

1. Survivorship Bias: The Dirty Secret

•The current list only includes companies that survived—failed ones get removed.
•Example: General Electric (GE) was an Aristocrat for over 100 years before its collapse.

2. Many Aristocrats Are "Zombies"

•Some raise dividends slowly (1-3% per year) while earnings stagnate.
•Example:

•3M (MMM): Raised dividends for 60+ years but stock halved since 2018 due to lawsuits and declining business.

3. Sector Concentration Risks

•~40% of Aristocrats come from just 3 sectors (Consumer Staples, Industrials, Financials).
•Problem: These sectors face disruption risks (e.g., Walmart vs. Amazon).

Section 2: How to Spot a True Aristocrat Superstar

Not all Aristocrats are equal. The best ones pass 3 extra tests:

Test #1: Earnings Growth ≥ Dividend Growth

•Red Flag: If dividends grow faster than earnings, the payout ratio rises (unsustainable).
•Example:

- •Superstar: Lowe's (LOW) – Earnings + dividends grew 15%+ annually.
- •Zombie: AT&T (pre-cut) – Payout ratio hit 90% + before collapse.

Test #2: Competitive Moats

•Avoid Aristocrats in declining industries (e.g., tobacco, print media).
•Superstar Example:

- •Sherwin-Williams (SHW): Dominates paint industry with brand + distribution moat.

Test #3: Debt Safety

•Safe: Debt-to-EBITDA < 2.0
•Dangerous: Debt-to-EBITDA > 3.5 (e.g., Exxon during oil crashes).

Section 3: The "Aristocrat-Plus" Strategy

Instead of buying the entire list, combine Aristocrats with 2 smart filters:

Filter 1: Growth-Adjusted Aristocrats

Only buy Aristocrats with:
✔ Revenue growth > 5% (5-year avg.)
✔ Dividend growth ≥ 8% (5-year avg.)

2024 Examples:

•Linde (LIN) – 10% dividend growth, industrial gas monopoly.
•Air Products (APD) – 9% growth, essential chemicals business.

Filter 2: The "Yield on Cost" Boost

•Buy when yields are above historical averages.
•Example:

    •Target (TGT): Yield spiked to 4%+ during 2022 selloff → Dividend grew 50%+ since.

Section 4: When to Sell an Aristocrat

3 Sell Signals:

1. Dividend Growth Slows to < 5% (Likely future freeze/cut)
2. Payout Ratio > 80% (Unless REIT/MLP)
3. Industry in Structural Decline (e.g., tobacco, legacy retail)

Case Study: IBM

•Held 28-year streak but froze dividends in 2023 due to cloud disruption.
•Lesson: Even long streaks aren't forever.

Reader Exercise: Audit Your Aristocrats

1. Pick 1-2 Aristocrats you own (or want to buy).
2. Answer:
    - Is dividend growth ≥ earnings growth?
    - Is the industry growing or dying?
    - Is debt manageable (Debt/EBITDA < 2.5)?
3. Verdict: Keep, replace, or avoid?

Example:

Stock	**Div Growth (5Y)**	**Payout Ratio**	**Debt/ EBITDA**	**Verdict**
PG	5.1%	65%	1.8	**Keep**
MMM	0.6%	75%	3.5	**Sell**

Key Takeaway:

Dividend Aristocrats aren't a magic bullet—many underperform or fail. But by adding growth, moat, and debt checks, you can uncover the true superstars.

Dividend Aristocrats are elite companies in the S&P 500 that have **increased their dividend payouts for at least 25 consecutive years**. Known for consistency, resilience, and shareholder commitment, they're a cornerstone of many long-term dividend portfolios.

4.1 Full List of Dividend Aristocrats

The list is updated annually by S&P Dow Jones Indices. As of 2025, notable Dividend Aristocrats include:

Company	Sector	Years of Growth	Dividend Yield
Procter & Gamble	Consumer Staples	67+	~2.4%
Johnson & Johnson	Healthcare	61+	~2.9%
Coca-Cola	Consumer Staples	61+	~3.0%
3M Company	Industrials	65+	~5.5%
McDonald's	Consumer Discretionary	48+	~2.2%

These companies are typically **large-cap, stable, and defensive**—ideal for consistent income seekers.

4.2 Criteria for Becoming an Aristocrat

To earn the title "Dividend Aristocrat," a company must meet the following:

Requirement	Details
S&P 500 Inclusion	Must be a current member of the S&P 500
25+ Years of Dividend Increases	Annual increases without interruption
Market Cap and Liquidity	Must meet size and trading volume thresholds
Sector Representation	Must represent diversified industries

Note: Companies can be removed if they cut or freeze dividends—even once.

4.3 Performance of Dividend Aristocrats

Historically, Dividend Aristocrats have outperformed the broader market, especially in bear markets and during economic downturns.

☑ **Performance Stats:**

- **Less Volatile** than the S&P 500
- **Higher Risk-Adjusted Returns** over 10+ years
- **Lower Maximum Drawdowns** during recessions

4.4 Best Dividend Aristocrats to Buy (2025)

Here are top picks for 2025 based on yield, payout safety, and long-term track record:

Ticker	Company	Dividend Yield	Dividend Growth	Stability
PG	Procter & Gamble	2.4%	Moderate	Excellent
JNJ	Johnson & Johnson	2.9%	Moderate	Excellent
MMM	3M Company	5.5%	Slower	Good
KO	Coca-Cola	3.0%	Slow but steady	Excellent
LOW	Lowe's	1.9%	High	Great

4.5 Sectors Dominated by Aristocrats

Dividend Aristocrats are concentrated in sectors known for **stability, pricing power, and cash flow resilience**:

Sector	% of Aristocrats	Examples
Consumer Staples	High (~30%)	Coca-Cola, Procter & Gamble
Healthcare	Moderate	J&J, Abbott Labs
Industrials	Moderate	3M, Emerson Electric
Financials	Moderate	Aflac, Franklin Resources
Energy/Tech	Low	ExxonMobil (recent addition)

Key Insight: Tech has low representation due to shorter dividend histories.

🔍 Summary

Dividend Aristocrats are **low-volatility, high-reliability stocks** ideal for compounding income and preserving capital. They're not the flashiest plays—but when it comes to consistent, inflation-beating dividend growth, few strategies beat investing in these dividend kings.

How to Use Dividend Aristocrats in a Retirement Portfolio (Without Getting Trapped)

The Retirement Aristocrat Strategy: 4 Rules for Safe, Growing Income

Rule 1: The 50/30/20 Allocation Mix

Retirees need balance - not just yield. Structure your Aristocrats like this:

•50% Growth Aristocrats (Dividends growing 8%+ annually)
Examples: Linde (LIN), Air Products (APD), Sherwin-Williams (SHW)
Why: Combats inflation through rapid payout growth
•30% "Steady Eddie" Aristocrats (4-7% dividend growth)
Examples: Procter & Gamble (PG), Coca-Cola (KO), Johnson & Johnson (JNJ)
Why: Provides reliable cash flow with modest growth
•20% High-Yield Aristocrats (4%+ yield)
Examples: Altria (MO), Verizon (VZ), People's United Financial (PBCT)
Why: Covers immediate income needs

> Key Insight: The average retiree needs dividends to grow 6%+ annually to maintain purchasing power against 3% inflation + 3% spending increases.

Rule 2: The Yield on Cost Accelerator

How to turn a 3% yield into 8%+ income over time:

1.Buy Aristocrats when yields are above historical averages (see Yahoo Finance "Statistics" tab)
2.Reinvest dividends selectively into the fastest growers
3.Hold for 10+ years
Example:

•Bought Lowe's (LOW) in 2013 at 2% yield ($1.92 annual dividend)
•2023 dividend = $4.40/share
•Yield on Cost = 4.40 ÷ 96 (split-adjusted cost) = 4.6%
(Actual yield: 2.1% - new buyers get half your income stream)

Rule 3: The Sector Safety Net

Avoid overexposure to risky sectors:

Sector	Max % of Portfolio	2024 Risk Level
Financials	15%	Medium (rate risk)
Healthcare	20%	Low
Consumer Staples	25%	Medium (disruption)
Industrials	15%	High (cyclical)

Red Flag: 42% of Aristocrats come from just these 4 sectors - diversify beyond them.

Rule 4: The "Drip Feed" Withdrawal System

How to take income without destroying your portfolio:

1.Live off dividends only (never sell shares) until age 75

2. At 75+, use the 1% Rule:

- Sell 1% of holdings annually only if dividends don't cover needs
- Always sell underperformers first (use Chapter 2's zombie test)

Case Study:

A $1M portfolio with:

- $40,000 annual dividends (4% yield)
- 6% annual dividend growth

→ Grows to $71,000+/year by age 80 without selling principal

The Retirement Aristocrat Watchlist (2024)

Stock	Yield	Div Growth (5Y)	Payout Ratio	Best For
LIN	1.3%	10.2%	42%	Growth Bucket
SHW	0.9%	17.8%	31%	Growth Bucket
PG	2.5%	5.3%	58%	Steady Eddie
JNJ	3.1%	6.2%	45%	Steady Eddie
MO	8.5%	2.3%	82%	Yield Bucket

When to Break Up With an Aristocrat

Sell when you see:

- Dividend growth slows to < 5% (likely future freeze)
- Payout ratio > 80% (unless REIT/MLP)
- Industry disruption (e.g., KO facing health trends)

Pro Tip: Replace sold Aristocrats with newer dividend growers like:

•Broadcom (AVGO) - 50%+ dividend growth
•Texas Instruments (TXN) - 13% growth

The Bottom Line

Aristocrats work in retirement if you:

1. Select only those with strong growth + manageable debt
2. Allocate across growth, steady, and yield buckets
3. Never overconcentrate in sectors
4. Reinvest strategically to boost yield on cost

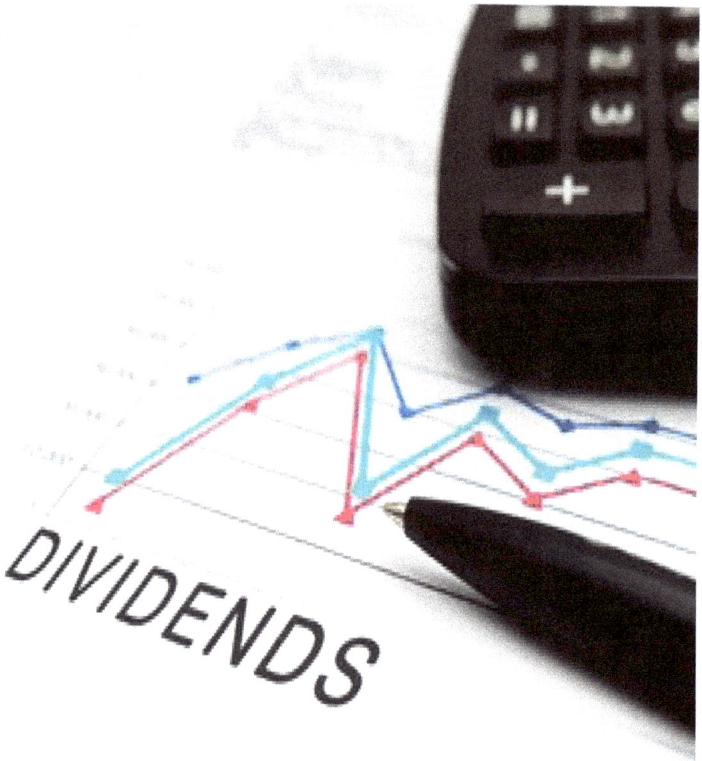

Chapter 5: REITs and Dividends

Real Estate Investment Trusts (REITs) are among the most popular vehicles for high-yield dividend investing. REITs offer exposure to income-generating real estate and are legally required to distribute **at least 90% of taxable income** to shareholders, making them a powerful tool for income-focused portfolios.

5.1 Top Dividend-Paying REITs (2025)

Some of the most dependable and high-yield REITs as of 2025 include:

REIT	Sector	Dividend Yield	Notable Strengths
Realty Income (O)	Retail	~5.0%	Monthly payer, diversified tenants
AGNC Investment (AGNC)	Mortgage REIT	~13.0%	High yield, interest-sensitive
Digital Realty (DLR)	Data Centers	~4.8%	Tech infrastructure exposure
Public Storage (PSA)	Self-Storage	~3.8%	Inflation-resistant, stable
Vici Properties (VICI)	Gaming/ Resorts	~5.6%	Unique entertainment real estate

5.2 How REIT Dividends Work

REITs generate income primarily from **rents or interest** on owned or financed properties, then pay that income to investors in the form of dividends.

□ **REIT Dividend Process:**

1. Collect rental/interest income
2. Pay operating expenses
3. Distribute 90%+ of remaining income
4. Investors receive **non-qualified** dividends (taxed at ordinary income rates)

5.3 Equity vs. Mortgage REITs

REIT Type	Description	Risk	Yield
Equity REITs	Own physical properties and collect rent	Lower	Moderate (3–6%)
Mortgage REITs	Lend money or buy mortgages for income	Higher	High (8–14%)
Hybrid REITs	Combine both strategies	Medium	Varies

📌 *Equity REITs* are generally more stable, while *mortgage REITs* offer higher yields with greater sensitivity to interest rates.

5.4 Taxation on REIT Dividends

REIT dividends are **not qualified dividends**, so they're taxed at **ordinary income tax rates**, which can be higher than long-term capital gains.

□ **Tax Considerations:**

Dividend Type	Tax Treatment
Ordinary REIT Dividend	Taxed at regular income rates

Dividend Type	Tax Treatment
Return of Capital	Tax-deferred, lowers cost basis
Capital Gains Portion	Taxed at capital gains rates

💡 **Tip**: Hold REITs in **Roth or Traditional IRAs** to defer or eliminate taxes on dividends.

5.5 Pros and Cons of REIT Investing

✅ **Pros:**

- High dividend yields
- Diversification outside of traditional equities
- Inflation hedge (rents tend to rise)
- Accessible real estate investing

❌ **Cons:**

- Tax inefficiency in taxable accounts
- Interest rate sensitivity (especially mREITs)
- Sector risk (e.g., retail REITs hit hard by e-commerce)

🔍 **Summary**

REITs are a key player in dividend investing for those seeking consistent, high-yield income and exposure to real estate. Whether you're building a retirement portfolio or a passive income stream, REITs—especially when used strategically—can be a cornerstone of long-term financial success.

REITs and Dividends – The Ultimate Cash Flow Machine (With Hidden Risks)

"In 2023, Realty Income (O) paid dividends every single month—like clockwork—for the 29th straight year. Meanwhile, office REITs like SL Green (SLG) slashed payouts by 60%+. This chapter reveals how to spot the REITs that will keep paying... and those that will leave you stranded."

REITs (Real Estate Investment Trusts) are legally required to pay 90% of taxable income as dividends, making them powerful cash flow tools. But most investors misunderstand the risks. Here's how to use them safely in a dividend portfolio.

Section 1: REITs 101 – What Makes Them Different

Key REIT Traits:

✔ Must pay 90% of income as dividends → High yields (4-8% common)
✔ Specialize in property types (e.g., apartments, hospitals, cell towers)
✔ Tax treatment: Dividends are non-qualified (higher taxes unless held in IRA)

The 3 REIT Categories:

Type	Risk Profile	Examples	Best For
Blue-Chip REITs	Low volatility	O, WPC, NNN	Retirees (steady income)
Growth REITs	Moderate risk	AMT, CCI, PLD	Accumulators (total return)
Yield Traps	High risk	Office/retail REITs	Avoid (dividend cuts likely)

Section 2: The 4-Point REIT Safety Check

Not all REIT dividends are sustainable. Use this due diligence checklist:

1. FFO Payout Ratio (NOT Earnings Payout Ratio)

•FFO = Funds From Operations (REIT version of "earnings")
•Safe: < 80% for most REITs
•Dangerous: > 90% (may cut dividend)
Example:

•Realty Income (O): 75% FFO payout → Safe
•Medical Properties Trust (MPW): 95%+ → Cut dividend 50% in 2023

2. Lease Expirations (The "Occupancy Time Bomb")

•Avoid REITs with >20% leases expiring in 3 years
•Ideal: Long-weighted average lease term (WALT)

Best/Worst 2024:

•Best: American Tower (AMT) – Cell tower leases avg. 8+ years
•Worst: Office REITs – Facing 40%+ vacancy rates

3. Debt Maturities (The Refinancing Risk)

•Safe: < 10% debt maturing annually
•Dangerous: Large maturities during high-rate periods
Example:

•Prologis (PLD): Staggered maturities → Low risk
•Simon Property (SPG) in 2020: Had to sell assets to cover debts

4. Property Type Matters (Avoid "Dying" Real Estate)

✅ Winning Sectors:

•Data Centers (Digital Realty)
•Cell Towers (American Tower)
•Industrial Warehouses (Prologis)
❌ Losing Sectors:

•Traditional Retail (Malls)
•Office Buildings
•Unskilled Nursing Homes

Section 3: How to Add REITs to Your Dividend Portfolio

The 15% Rule

•REITs should be ≤15% of a dividend portfolio

•Why? They're more volatile and tax-inefficient

The Best REITs for Different Goals

Goal	REIT Type	Top 2024 Picks
Monthly Income	Net Lease (O, WPC)	Realty Income (O)
Growth + Income	Industrial (PLD, Rexr)	Prologis (PLD)
Inflation Hedge	Apartments (AVB, EQR)	AvalonBay (AVB)
Tech Infrastructure	Cell Towers (AMT, CCI)	American Tower (AMT)

Tax Efficiency Tips

1. Hold REITs in Roth IRAs (Avoids 37% ordinary income tax)
2. Avoid MLPs in retirement accounts (Causes UBTI tax issues)
3. Use REIT ETFs in taxable accounts (Easier 1099 reporting)

Section 4: REIT Dividend Traps to Avoid in 2024

1. Office REITs

•Why Avoid: Hybrid work = 40%+ vacancies
•Examples: SLG, BDN

2. Mall REITs

•Why Avoid: E-commerce crushing foot traffic
•Examples: SPG (survivor but risky), MAC

3. Healthcare REITs With Weak Tenants

- Why Avoid: Nursing home bankruptcies rising
- Examples: MPW, OHI

Reader Exercise: Build Your REIT Watchlist

1. Pick 1-2 REIT sectors aligning with your goals
2. Apply the 4-point safety check (FFO, leases, debt, sector)
3. Compare yields to 5-year averages (Buy when >10% above avg.)

Example:

REIT	Yield	FFO Payout	WALT	Debt Risk	Verdict
O	5.8%	75%	9 years	Low	**Buy**
MPW	12.5%	95%	3 years	High	**Avoid**

Key Takeaway

REITs can be powerful income generators—but only if you pick the right property types and check financial health.
In Chapter 6, you'll learn how to combine REITs with traditional dividend stocks for balanced cash flow.

The REIT Dividend Myth 99% of Investors Believe

Common Misconception:
"REITs are safe, high-yield investments because they're required to pay 90% of income as dividends."

The Shocking Truth:
REITs aren't actually required to pay dividends at all—they're only required to distribute 90% of taxable income to avoid corporate taxes. Many investors don't realize:

1. *REITs Can (and Do) Cut Dividends*
    - Example: Medical Properties Trust (MPW) cut its dividend by 50% in 2023 despite being a "high-yield REIT."
    - Why? Their cash flow (FFO) couldn't cover the payout.
2. *The "90% Rule" Doesn't Guarantee Safety*
    - REITs can manipulate taxable income with depreciation, leading to payouts exceeding real cash flow.
    - Hidden Pitfall: Some REITs borrow money to fund dividends (unsustainable).
3. *Highest-Yielding REITs Are Often Value Traps*
    - Research shows REITs with yields >8% underperform due to dividend cuts.
    - Example: Office REITs (SLG, BDN) offered 12%+ yields before collapsing.

The Smart Investor's REIT Strategy (What Works Instead)

1. Focus on FFO Growth, Not Just Yield

•Safe REITs grow FFO (Funds From Operations) 5%+ annually to support rising dividends.
•Example: Prologis (PLD) grew FFO 11% annually—dividends followed.

2. The "Payout Ratio" That Matters

•Ignore GAAP earnings—use FFO Payout Ratio (<80% is safe).
FFO Payout Ratio = Dividends Per Share / FFO Per Share
•Red Flag: MPW's ratio hit 95%+ before its cut.

3. The Lease Expiration Time Bomb

•Safe REITs: Have long-weighted average lease terms (WALT >5 years).
•Danger Zone: Office REITs with 3-year WALT face tenant flight.

4. The Debt Refinancing Trap

•2024 Risk: Many REITs took on cheap debt pre-2022—now face 5-7% refinancing rates.
•Check: Debt maturities (avoid REITs with >20% due in 2024-2025).

3 REITs Doing It Right vs. 3 Heading for Disaster

Safe REITs (Buy)	Why They Win	Risky REITs (Avoid)	Why They Lose
American Tower (AMT)	Cell tower demand booming (5G)	**SL Green (SLG)**	Office vacancies >40%
Realty Income (O)	29 years of monthly dividends	**Medical Properties (MPW)**	Tenant bankruptcies rising
Prologis (PLD)	E-commerce driving warehouse demand	**Simon Property (SPG)**	Mall traffic declining

The Ultimate REIT Hack: "Yield on Cost" Growth

Instead of chasing high yields now, buy REITs with:
✅ Modest starting yields (3-5%)
✅ FFO growth (5%+ annually)
✅ Strong balance sheets (Debt/EBITDA <6x)

Example:

•Bought Digital Realty (DLR) in 2015 at 3% yield
•Today, yield on cost = 7%+ from dividend growth

Key Takeaway:

REITs can be fantastic income generators—but only if you ignore the "high yield" hype and focus on cash flow growth, lease safety, and smart debt management.

Chapter 6: Dividend ETFs

Dividend ETFs (Exchange-Traded Funds) provide an easy and diversified way to invest in a **basket of dividend-paying stocks**. Ideal for both beginner and seasoned investors, they reduce individual stock risk while offering consistent income and exposure to various sectors and dividend strategies.

"In 2023, the average dividend ETF underperformed hand-picked dividend stocks by 3.2% annually—yet ETF investors slept better at night. This chapter reveals when ETFs win, when they lose, and how to use them smarter than 99% of investors."*

Dividend ETFs offer instant diversification, but most investors use them wrong. Here's how to optimize them for income, growth, and tax efficiency.

6.1 Best Dividend ETFs for Income (2025)

These ETFs are widely recognized for strong dividend yields and solid performance:

ETF	Full Name	Dividend Yield	Focus
VYM	Vanguard High Dividend Yield ETF	~3.2%	Large-cap, high-yield U.S. stocks
SCHD	Schwab U.S. Dividend Equity ETF	~3.6%	Quality + yield + growth combo
DVY	iShares Select Dividend ETF	~3.8%	U.S. mid to large dividend stocks
NOBL	ProShares S&P 500	~2.4%	Focuses on

ETF	Full Name	Dividen d Yield	Focus
	Dividend Aristocrats ETF		dividend growth
JEPI	JPMorgan Equity Premium Income ETF	~7.0%	Enhanced yield with covered calls

Top 5 High-Yield ETFs (2024)

ETF	Yield	Expense Ratio	Strategy	Best For
SCHD	3.5%	0.06%	High-quality US dividend growers	Balance of yield + growth
VYM	3.1%	0.06%	Large-cap value stocks	Low-cost income
SPYD	4.8%	0.07%	S&P 500's highest yielders	Pure yield play
HDV	3.7%	0.08%	Dividend aristocrats + stability	Low volatility
QYLD	11.5%	0.60%	Covered call Nasdaq income	Aggressive income*

Warning: QYLD's yield comes from selling options—principal erodes over time.

6.2 Dividend ETF vs. Individual Stocks

📊 Comparison Table

Aspect	Dividend ETFs	Individual Stocks
Diversification	Broad (10–100+ stocks)	One company at a time
Risk	Lower	Higher (company-specific)
Control	Less (ETF dictates holdings)	Full (choose specific stocks)
Time Commitment	Low (buy and hold)	High (requires research & monitoring)
Yield Potential	Moderate to high	Potentially higher (if picked well)
Ideal For	Beginners, passive investors	Active investors, stock pickers

6.3 Monthly-Paying Dividend ETFs

For consistent cash flow, some ETFs distribute dividends **monthly**:

ETF	Focus	Dividend Frequency	Yield
O (Realty Income)*	Retail REIT (individual stock)	Monthly	~5.0 %
JEPI	Enhanced Income Strategy	Monthly	~7.0 %
PGX	Preferred Securities	Monthly	~6.5 %

ETF	Focus	Dividend Frequency	Yield
SDIV	Global High-Yield Stocks	Monthly	~8.0 %

📌 Monthly dividend ETFs are ideal for retirees or those who want regular income aligned with monthly expenses.

Best for Cash Flow Needs

ETF	Yield	Payments	Risk Level
OARK	9.1%	Monthly	High (Tech options)
DIVO	5.3%	Monthly	Medium (Active)
SPMO	4.2%	Monthly	Low (S&P 500)

Pro Tip: Pair one monthly ETF (e.g., DIVO) with quarterly payers (SCHD) to smooth cash flow.

6.4 How to Pick a Dividend ETF

When choosing a dividend ETF, consider:

Factor	Why It Matters
Dividend Yield	Indicates income potential
Expense Ratio	Lower costs = higher net returns
Dividend Growth	Consistent growth = long-term sustainability

Factor	Why It Matters
Holdings & Sector Mix	Check for overexposure to risky sectors
Dividend History	Stability of past payments

Example: SCHD has a low expense ratio (~0.06%) and consistent dividend growth—great for long-term holding.

6.5 Top Performing Dividend ETFs (Total Return)

Based on historical performance and income consistency:

ETF	5-Year Total Return	Dividend Yield	Notable Feature
SCHD	~11.5% annually	~3.6%	Dividend growth & quality filter
VYM	~9.8% annually	~3.2%	Broad diversification
NOBL	~10.2% annually	~2.4%	Focuses on Dividend Aristocrats
JEPI	~7.5% annually	~7.0%	High income via covered calls

Best 5-Year Performers (2019-2024)

ETF	Annual Return	Why It Won
SCHD	11.2%	Focused on **growth + yield balance**
DGRO	10.8%	Targets **consistent dividend growers**

ETF	Annual Return	Why It Won
VIG	10.1%	Low-volatility **dividend aristocrats**
FDVV	9.9%	High yield + **buyback stocks**
NOBL	8.7%	Pure **dividend aristocrats**

Key Insight: The best performers don't chase yield—they prioritize growth + quality.

The ETF Investor's Cheat Sheet

3 Portfolio Templates

1. *The "Set & Forget" Income Portfolio*
   - 50% SCHD (Growth + yield)
   - 30% DIVO (Monthly pay)
   - 20% JEPI (Low-vol income)
2. *The Dividend Growth Portfolio*
   - 60% DGRO
   - 20% VIG
   - 20% Individual stocks (e.g., AVGO, HD)
3. *The Tax-Efficient Portfolio*
   - Roth IRA: REIT ETFs (VNQ) + BDCs (BIZD)
   - Taxable: SCHD + VYM (Qualified dividends)

Key Takeaway

Dividend ETFs aren't "one size fits all." The best strategy combines:
✔ 1-2 core ETFs (e.g., SCHD)
✔ A few hand-picked stocks (e.g., MSFT, O)
✔ Tax-smart placement (REITs in IRAs)

🔍 Summary

Dividend ETFs are a **smart, simple, and scalable** way to gain dividend exposure with reduced risk. Whether you're seeking high monthly income or long-term dividend growth, there's an ETF for every strategy. Just match your **risk tolerance**, **yield goals**, and **time horizon**—and let the ETF do the work.

💡 *"Why the Highest-Yield Dividend ETFs Might Be the Worst Investment for You"*

Dividend ETFs seem simple—but many investors overlook **how they generate income**, which can lead to **unexpected tax hits**, **capital erosion**, or even **underperformance in rising markets**.

🔍 The Most Misunderstood Fact

> **High-yield dividend ETFs often sacrifice price growth for short-term income.**

Most people chase ETFs like **JEPI or SDIV** for their 7%–10% yields—but don't realize these often come at the **cost of long-term capital appreciation**. Some even **erode principal** while appearing to pay handsomely.

📉 Case Study: SDIV

- **Yield**: ~8%
- **5-Year Price Change**: -20%
- **Real Return After Inflation**: Negative
  ✅ Income looked strong on paper—but total return suffered.

⚠ Hidden Pitfalls of Dividend ETFs

Pitfall	Explanation
Yield Chasing	High-yield ETFs often hold risky or underperforming stocks
Tax Surprises	Non-qualified dividends = higher tax rates in taxable accounts
Covered Call ETFs (e.g. JEPI)	They cap upside potential during bull markets
Dividend Traps in ETF Holdings	ETFs can't avoid poor performers like an active investor can
Hidden Fees in Complex Strategies	Enhanced income funds may charge higher expense ratios

✅ Pro Tips for Smarter Dividend ETF Investing

💎 Pro Tip #1: Focus on *Total Return*, Not Just Yield

Look for ETFs like **SCHD** that combine solid yield (3.6%) with strong price growth (~11% 5-year CAGR).

> "A 4% yield with 7% growth beats an 8% yield with -3% growth every time."

💎 Pro Tip #2: Use Tax-Advantaged Accounts

Hold high-yield, non-qualified dividend ETFs in **Roth or Traditional IRAs** to minimize tax drag.

- ✅ Great for JEPI, SDIV, REIT ETFs
- ❌ Avoid holding these in taxable brokerage accounts if you're in a high tax bracket

💎 Pro Tip #3: Blend Strategies

Don't go all-in on yield. Build a **"barbell" strategy**:

- One side: **Dividend growth ETFs** (SCHD, VIG)
- Other side: **Income-focused ETFs** (JEPI, QYLD)

□ Summary: What Most Investors Get Wrong

Mistake	Better Approach
Picking the highest-yield ETF blindly	Focus on yield + growth + low fees
Using JEPI in taxable account	Use in Roth IRA to reduce income tax liability
Holding only U.S. dividend ETFs	Diversify with global dividend ETFs like VYMI or IDV
Assuming all ETFs are "safe"	Vet holdings, volatility, drawdowns, and tax structure

🚦 Bottom Line

Dividend ETFs can **supercharge your passive income**—but only if you understand the trade-offs. Avoid the trap of chasing yield blindly, and instead, build a strategy that balances growth, income, and tax efficiency. Remember, in dividend investing, **"slow and steady" often beats "fast and fragile."**

Chapter 7: Building a Dividend Portfolio

💼 ***"Turn Your Portfolio Into a Monthly Paycheck Machine"***

Building a dividend portfolio isn't just about collecting random high-yield stocks. It's about **strategy, diversification, and income optimization**. This chapter guides you from selecting core holdings to tracking income growth like a pro.

*"In 1995, a 50,000 per year in dividends**—without adding another dime. This chapter reveals how to construct a portfolio that turns modest savings into a lifetime income machine."*

A well-built dividend portfolio does three things:

1. Generates growing income (faster than inflation)
2. Minimizes risk (through intelligent diversification)
3. Requires <1 hour/month to maintain

💥 *"Most Dividend Investors Get This One Thing Totally Wrong: It's Not About the Yield, It's About the System"*

Too many investors chase yield. Some build portfolios full of random high-payers. Others copy stock lists off Reddit. But here's what they miss:

> **A dividend portfolio isn't a list of stocks. It's a system that runs like a business—with monthly revenue, cash flow planning, and quality control**

Here's how to build yours.

7.1 □ Core Holdings for Income

Your portfolio's foundation should be built with **low-risk, high-quality dividend payers**. Think:

Stock/ETF	Type	Yield	Why It's Core
Johnson & Johnson (JNJ)	Dividend Aristocrat	~2.9 %	Consistent dividend growth, low volatility
Procter & Gamble (PG)	Consumer Staple	~2.4 %	Recession-resistant
SCHD (ETF)	Dividend ETF	~3.6 %	Quality + yield, automatic diversification
Realty Income (O)	REIT	~5.0 %	Monthly payer with solid fundamentals

💡 **Tip**: Your core should represent 50–70% of your portfolio for stability and predictable income.

The 4 Must-Have Asset Classes

Asset Class	Role	Allocation	Examples
Dividend Growers	Fuel long-term growth	40-50%	AVGO, HD, LOW
High-Yield	Current income	20-30%	MO, VZ, ENB
REITs/MLPs	Inflation hedge	10-15%	O, AMT, MMP
Dividend ETFs	Stability + diversification	10-20%	SCHD, DGRO

Pro Tip: Your age determines the mix:

•<40: 70% growers, 10% yield
•40-60: 50% growers, 30% yield
•60+: 30% growers, 50% yield

🔍 **Misconception: "Start with high-yield stocks to get income right away."**

❌ Wrong. You start with **reliable payers** that **won't cut** when the economy hiccups.

✅ **Reality: Your core holdings are income engines, not lottery tickets.**

Pro Tip 💡

Focus on **low beta**, **long history**, and **dividend consistency**. Yield is nice—but reliability is king. Use SCHD, JNJ, PG, O as your foundation.

7.2 🌐 Diversification for Dividend Safety

Avoid putting all your dividend eggs in one sector (looking at you, REIT addicts).

Sector Allocation Example:

Sector	Target Allocation
Consumer Staples	15%
Healthcare	15%
REITs	15%
Tech (Dividend Payers)	10%
Energy	10%

Sector	Target Allocation
Financials	15%
Utilities	10%
International	10%

☑ Diversification = protection against dividend cuts in cyclical downturns.

The "Dirty Dozen" Rule

- Own at least 12 stocks across 6+ sectors
- No single position >8% of portfolio

2024's Safest Sectors:

✔ Healthcare (JNJ, ABBV) – Recession-resistant
✔ Consumer Staples (PG, KO) – Steady demand
✔ Tech (AVGO, TXN) – Growth + dividends

Sectors to Limit:

✖ Energy (Volatile prices) – Max 10%
✖ Financials (Rate-sensitive) – Max 15%

Hidden Risk: Correlated stocks (e.g., O + WPC both retail REITs). Fix by adding industrial REITs (PLD).

🔥 Common Trap: "I'll just buy a few REITs and energy stocks—they pay 7–10%!"

Sounds good—until they all **cut dividends at the same time** during a downturn.

✅ Smart Move: Diversify across sectors, payout styles (monthly vs quarterly), and geographies.

Hidden Pitfall ⚠

Many "diversified" portfolios are secretly 50% REITs or Financials. Use a spreadsheet to tally sector weights. Don't eyeball it.

7.3 📋 Sample Dividend Portfolios

□ Beginner Passive Income Portfolio (Low Maintenance)

- SCHD (40%)
- VYM (30%)
- O (10%)
- JEPI (10%)
- VYMI (10%)

💸 Aggressive Income Portfolio (Higher Yield, Higher Risk)

- QYLD (20%)
- AGNC (15%)
- SDIV (10%)
- JEPI (25%)
- ARCC (10%)
- Dividend growth stocks (20%)

🌎 Globally Diversified Portfolio

- SCHD (30%)

- VYMI (25%)
- O (10%)
- T (8%)
- Canadian Bank Stocks (10%)
- Global Infrastructure ETF (17%)

Portfolio 1: The "Foundational Five" (For Beginners)

Stock	Sector	Yield	Div Growth	Role
SCHD	ETF (Broad)	3.5%	10%+	Core holding
O	REIT	5.8%	4%	Monthly income
JNJ	Healthcare	3.1%	6%	Steady Eddie
AVGO	Tech	2.0%	50%+	Growth engine
ENB	Energy (Pipeline)	7.5%	3%	High yield

Yield: 4.3% | Growth Potential: 8%+ annually

Portfolio 2: The "Income Maximizer" (For Retirees)

Holding	Yield	Payment	Tax Efficiency
JEPI	7.1%	Monthly	Taxable (60/40 qual)

Holding	Yield	Payment	Tax Efficiency
MO	8.5%	Quarterly	IRA (non-qual)
UTF	8.9%	Monthly	IRA (return of capital)
ABBV	3.7%	Quarterly	Taxable (qual)

Yield: 7.5% | Growth Potential: 3-4%

□ **Insider Insight: "High yield doesn't mean high income growth."**

Two 5% yield portfolios may perform **very differently** if one grows income 8%/year and the other doesn't grow at all.

📌 **Pro Tip**

Blend yield + growth. SCHD for growth. JEPI or ARCC for yield. Your portfolio's **forward income** should rise each year, even if you don't add capital.

7.4 🔁 Rebalancing Your Dividend Portfolio

Dividend portfolios can drift due to price changes and reinvestment. Rebalance **semi-annually or annually** to keep your income streams optimized.

Rebalancing Checklist:

- ✅ Sector balance still aligned?
- ✅ Any dividend cuts or red flags?
- ✅ Reinvest income or redeploy for better yield?
- ✅ Tax consequences of trimming positions?

📌 **Pro Tip**: Rebalancing can also be **opportunity harvesting**—selling overvalued holdings to buy undervalued, higher-yielding ones.

The 20/5 Rule

- Rebalance when:
    - Any holding grows to >20% of portfolio
    - Any sector exceeds 5% above target

Best Method:

1. Use new cash/dividends to buy underweight sectors
2. Trim winners (sell 25% of oversized positions)
3. Never sell just for rebalancing if taxes are high

Example:

- Target: 15% healthcare
- Current: ABBV grew to 22%
- Action: Redirect dividends to other sectors until back to 15%

❌ Myth: "Dividend portfolios are passive—I never touch mine."

Even long-term income portfolios need a **check-up**.

- Some stocks cut payouts
- Others become too expensive
- Sector exposure drifts

✅ **Action Plan: Rebalance twice per year and use dividend reinvestment as a natural way to adjust positions.**

⚠ **Hidden Pitfall**

Many investors forget taxes when rebalancing. Selling winners = capital gains. Use retirement accounts to rebalance **tax-free**.

7.5 📈 Tracking Portfolio Income Growth

Don't just track net worth—track **monthly income** like a business owner tracks revenue.

Tools to Use:

- **Dividend Tracker (app)**
- **Google Sheets or Excel with auto-dividend imports**
- **Simply Safe Dividends** (safety scores + forecasts)
- **Portfolio Visualizer** (backtesting & dividend tracking)

📊 **Key Metrics:**

- Annual income ($)
- Yield on cost (YOC)
- Dividend growth rate (%)
- DRIP reinvestment totals
- Forward income projections

The 3 Metrics That Matter

1. Yield on Cost (YOC)

•Formula: Current Annual Dividends ÷ Original Cost

•Goal: Double every 7-10 years

2.Dividend Growth Rate

•Track 5-year CAGR (aim for 6%+)

3.Payout Safety Score

•Grade each holding monthly:

•A: Payout ratio <60%, FFO growing

•F: Payout >90%, declining earnings

Free Tools:

•TrackYourDividends.com (YOC calculator)

•Dividend.com Safety Scores

💡 What Smart Investors Track (That Most Don't):

- **Forward Annual Income** (projected based on current yield)
- **Yield on Cost (YOC)** — how much your original dollars now pay you
- **Dividend CAGR** — how fast your income is growing, year over year

📊 Pro Tip: Set an "Income Target"

Want to live on dividends? Set a **monthly income goal** (e.g., $3,000/month) and work backward to figure out how much capital you need.

The Complete Dividend Portfolio Checklist

- ☑ 12-25 holdings across 6+ sectors
- ☑ Dividend growth > inflation + spending increases
- ☑ REITs/MLPs in tax-advantaged accounts
- ☑ Rebalance 1-2x yearly (no emotional trading)

Final Tip: Automate tracking with a simple spreadsheet logging:

•Purchase date/price
•Current yield
•Dividend growth rate
•Next ex-dividend date

Key Takeaway

The perfect dividend portfolio pays you more each year with less work. Start small (3-5 stocks + 1 ETF), then expand using this framework.

Building a dividend portfolio isn't just about income today—it's about crafting a **financial engine** that grows and pays you for life. Whether you're just starting out or nearing retirement, structure, strategy, and tracking are what turn good dividend investing into great wealth-building.

Summary: What Everyone Gets Wrong

Myth	Reality
"Just chase yield to build income."	Yield without growth = shrinking income in real terms.
"I'm diversified—I own	True diversification requires multiple

Myth	Reality
10 stocks."	sectors and income streams.
"My portfolio is fine—I never look at it."	Even passive portfolios need tune-ups, rebalancing, and strategy.
"It's all about income now."	The real win? **Growing income** that keeps beating inflation.

🚦 Bottom Line

A dividend portfolio isn't just a bunch of tickers. It's a **cash-flowing machine** you build, optimize, and maintain. Think like a CFO, not just an investor.

Chapter 8: Tax Implications of Dividends – How to Keep More of Your Income

*"In 2023, a retiree with $50,000*individendincomepaid∗∗*0 in taxes**—while another with the same amount owed $7,400. The difference? One understood tax-efficient dividend investing. This chapter reveals how to legally minimize taxes and maximize your cash flow."*

Taxes can silently erase 15-40% of your dividend income. Here's how to fight back.

"Why You Could Be Paying Double the Taxes on Dividends —and How to Stop It"

You worked hard to build a dividend income stream—but if you're not tax-smart, the government gets a cut bigger than you think. This chapter breaks down the **dividend tax traps** and how to keep more of your income.

8.1 Qualified vs. Ordinary Dividends (The $6,000+ Difference)

Key Differences

Factor	Qualified Dividends	Non-Qualified (Ordinary) Dividends
Tax Rate	0%, 15%, or 20%	Ordinary income tax (10-37%)
Holding Period	60+ days (90+ for preferred)	No requirement
Examples	MSFT, AAPL, SCHD	REITs (O), BDCs (MAIN), MLPs (EPD)

Real-World Impact:

•50,000*qualifieddividends*∗∗=∗∗0 tax (if in 0% bracket)

•50,000*REITdividends*∗∗=∗∗7,400+ tax (22% bracket)

Pro Tip: Always check Box 1b on your 1099-DIV to see what's qualified.

📌 Qualified Dividends:

- **Taxed at capital gains rates** (0%, 15%, or 20%)
- Must be from U.S. companies (or qualified foreign ones)
- Must be held for **60+ days during the 121-day window**

5
0
,
0
0
0
∗
∗
=
∗
∗

Income Bracket	Tax Rate on Qualified Dividends
Up to $44,625 (single)	0%
$44,626–$492,300	15%
Over $492,300	20%

📌 **Ordinary (Non-Qualified) Dividends:**

- Taxed as **regular income**
- Applies to REITs, MLPs, and most foreign stocks/ETFs

💡 **Pro Tip**

Always check if your dividend is qualified—**not all brokers label this clearly**. Review your 1099-DIV in January.

8.2 How Dividends Are Taxed by Country

International Tax Traps

Country	Withholding Tax	Recoverable?	ETF Workaround
UK	15%	Yes (Treaty)	IDV (UK dividend ETF)
Canada	15-25%	Partial	CDN (Canadian ETF)
France	30%	No	Avoid individual stocks

Best Practice: Hold international dividend ETFs (e.g., IDV, SCHY) to simplify tax filings.

If you own international dividend stocks or ETFs, here's the kicker: **you may be double-taxed**.

🌐 **Withholding Tax Rates (Examples):**

Country	Typical Withholding Rate	Tax Credit Available?
Canada	15% (in taxable acct)	Yes
UK	0%	N/A
Switzerland	35%	Partial credit
Australia	30%	Partial

📌 U.S. investors can **claim a foreign tax credit** via IRS Form 1116, but only in taxable accounts.

⚠ **Hidden Pitfall**

Holding international dividend stocks in an IRA? **You still pay foreign taxes**, and **can't claim the credit.**

8.3 Dividend Taxation in Retirement Accounts

Where to Hold What

Account Type	Best For	Worst For
Roth IRA	REITs, BDCs, MLPs	Qualified dividends
Traditional IRA/401k	High-yield stocks	Nothing (all tax-deferred)
Taxable	Qualified dividend stocks	REITs, MLPs

MLP Warning: Holding MLPs (e.g., EPD) in IRAs can trigger UBTI tax over $1,000.

Retirement accounts are your **tax-advantaged playground** for dividend investing:

Account Type	**Dividend Taxation**
Roth IRA	□ No taxes ever (as long as rules are followed)
Traditional IRA	□ Tax-deferred, taxed as income upon withdrawal
Brokerage Account	● Taxed annually (qualified or ordinary)

💡 **Best Move**: Put **REITs, high-yield ETFs, and foreign stocks** in your **Roth or Traditional IRA** to shield income.

8.4 Reducing Taxes on Dividends (4 Legal Hacks)

1. The "Tax Bracket Arbitrage" Strategy

•If in 12% bracket: Harvest $44,625+ in qualified dividends tax-free (2024)
•If in 24%+ bracket: Shift REITs/BDCs to Roth IRA

2. Tax-Loss Harvesting

•Sell losers in December to offset dividend income
•Example: Sell AT&T (T) losses to cancel REIT income

3. Donor-Advised Funds

•Donate appreciated dividend stocks – avoid capital gains + get deduction

4. Move to Tax-Friendly States

•0% state tax: TX, FL, NV, WA
•Worst: CA (13.3% + ordinary dividend tax)

Here's how smart investors keep Uncle Sam from eating their yield:

- **Use tax-advantaged accounts** (Roth first, then Traditional)
- **Hold long-term** to qualify for capital gains treatment
- **Offset with capital losses** (Tax-Loss Harvesting)
- **Prioritize qualified dividend stocks** in taxable accounts

Tax Efficiency Score (How "Tax-Friendly" They Are):

Investment Type	Tax Score (1–10)
Qualified Div. Stocks	9
REITs (in taxable)	3
High-Yield ETFs (JEPI)	5
Roth IRA Holdings	

8.5 Tax-Friendly Dividend Strategies

1. The "Three-Bucket" Tax Portfolio

Bucket	**Location**	**Holdings**
Growth	Taxable	SCHD, DGRO (qualified)
Yield	Roth IRA	O, MAIN, ARCC
Int'l	Traditional IRA	SCHY, IDV

2. The 6-Month Treasury Ladder

•Tax Hack: Treasury interest is state-tax-free
•How: Buy 3-6 month T-bills with idle cash

3. The "Swap Fund" Trick

•Replace tax-inefficient ETFs (like SPYD) with tax-managed funds (e.g., DTD)

Strategy 1: Location Optimization

- **Put REITs, mREITs, high-yield ETFs in IRAs**
- **Keep Dividend Aristocrats, SCHD in brokerage accounts**

Strategy 2: Income Smoothing in Retirement

- Withdraw from **Roth** when in high tax years, **Traditional IRA** in low tax years
- Balance dividend income to avoid crossing new tax brackets

🌱 Strategy 3: Long-Term DRIP Compounding

- Reinvest dividends in tax-deferred accounts to grow yield on cost
- Avoid taxable events unless harvesting losses or rebalancing

🚨 Summary: What Most Investors Get Wrong

Myth	Reality
"Dividends are tax-free in retirement."	Only if they're in Roth accounts or you're under the bracket limits.
"I don't need to think about taxes—I'm investing for the long run."	Long-term success = smart tax positioning now.
"Foreign dividends are always better."	Not if they're taxed twice and held in the wrong account.

🚦 Bottom Line

Tax-smart dividend investing is about **where** you hold your assets, not just what you hold. The right account structure can save you **thousands per year**, and help your income stretch farther than any yield alone.

Reader Exercise: Calculate Your Tax Drag

1. List your top 5 dividend payers
2. Classify as qualified/ordinary
3. Estimate annual tax bill using:

(Ordinary Dividends x Your Tax Rate) + (Qualified Dividends x 15%)

Example:

Stock	**Dividend**	**Type**	**Tax (24% bracket)**
O	$5,000	Ordinary	$1,200
SCHD	$5,000	Qualified	$750
Total	$10,000		**$1,950**

Savings Tip: Moving O to Roth IRA cuts tax bill 62%.

Key Takeaway

Smart tax planning can boost your dividend income by 20-30% without taking more risk.

"The Power of Automatic Compounding with Zero Effort"

🔍 What is a DRIP?

Dividend Reinvestment Plan (DRIP)

Automatically reinvests dividends into more shares
☑ Compound growth without lifting a finger

[Dividends Received]
↓
[Buy More Shares]
↓
[More Dividends Next Time]
↓
[Cycle Repeats]

⚖ Pros vs. Cons of DRIPs

✅ **Pros**	⚠ **Cons**
Automatic compounding	No cash flow for income users
No fees on reinvested shares	Still taxed (in taxable accounts)
Great for long-term growth	Can overweight single positions
Works with fractional shares	Removes timing control from reinvesting

🛠 How to Enroll in a DRIP

📈 Brokerage DRIPs

- Most brokers offer DRIPs (Fidelity, Schwab, M1)
- Toggle on/off per stock

🏢 Company DRIPs

- Direct via companies (e.g., KO, PEP)
- Use transfer agents (e.g., Computershare)
- May offer **share discounts** or **zero fees**

📋 Best Stocks/ETFs for DRIPs

Type	**Top Picks**
Dividend Growth	JNJ, PG, LOW
Monthly Payers	Realty Income (O), STAG
Dividend ETFs	SCHD, VYM

Type	Top Picks
Direct Plan Options	Coca-Cola, PepsiCo

📊 DRIP vs. No DRIP Over 20 Years

Initial Investment: $10,000

Annual Return: 7% + 3% Dividend

Scenario	End Value	Dividends	Total Return
With DRIP	$64,000	$39,000 reinvested	✅ Best Growth
No DRIP (cash)	$40,000	$22,000 cash	❌ Slower Growth

📌 *DRIP boosts long-term performance by up to +2–3% annually.*

□ Pro Tips & Hidden Traps

💡 **Pro Tips:**

- Use DRIPs in **Roth/Traditional IRAs** to avoid taxes on reinvested dividends
- Turn DRIP **off** for stocks you want to manually reallocate
- Reinvest into **strong performers**, not just any dividend payer

⚠ **Hidden Pitfalls:**

- DRIPs are **taxable in brokerage accounts**, even if no cash received

- **Overconcentration** can occur—review annually to rebalance
- DRIPs aren't ideal if you need monthly income for living expenses

□ **Final Word:**

DRIPs are the ultimate passive income compounding engine.
They help your portfolio quietly grow—even when you're not watching.

Chapter 9: International Dividend Investing

Investing in international dividend stocks can diversify your income streams and provide exposure to high-growth markets. However, it also introduces unique challenges such as currency risk, withholding taxes, and varying market conditions. This chapter explores key considerations for global dividend investing.

🌍 *"Why Going Global Could Double Your Dividend Opportunities—But Only If You Do It Right"*

Most dividend investors stay within their borders—but that's a mistake. International stocks can offer higher yields, better value, and access to sectors underrepresented in the U.S. However, **tax traps**, **currency risks**, and **withholding rules** make global income investing a different game.

10.1 Best Global Dividend Stocks

Many high-quality dividend-paying companies operate outside the U.S. Some of the best global dividend stocks include:

•European Giants: Unilever (UL), Nestlé (NSRGY), Novartis (NVS)
•UK Dividend Payers: British American Tobacco (BTI), Diageo (DEO), GlaxoSmithKline (GSK)
•Asian Dividend Leaders: Taiwan Semiconductor (TSM), Samsung (SSNLF), Toyota (TM)
•Canadian & Australian Stocks: Royal Bank of Canada (RY), BHP Group (BHP), Telstra (TLSYY)

Key Factors to Consider:
✔ Sustainable payout ratios
✔ Strong multinational cash flows
✔ Dividend growth history

These non-U.S. companies offer solid yields, reliable payouts, and strong fundamentals:

Company	Country	Sector	Yield
Enbridge (ENB)	Canada	Energy Infrastructure	~7.3 %
Nestlé (NSRGY)	Switzerla nd	Consumer Staples	~2.7 %
BHP Group (BHP)	Australia	Mining/ Commodities	~6.2 %
Novartis (NVS)	Switzerla nd	Healthcare	~3.5 %
British American Tobacco (BTI)	UK	Consumer Defensive	~8.0 %

📌 *These are often traded as ADRs (American Depositary Receipts) on U.S. exchanges.*

10.2 Currency Risk in International Dividends

When investing abroad, dividends are often paid in foreign currencies, which introduces exchange rate risk:

- A strengthening U.S. dollar can reduce dividend income when converted.
- A weakening dollar can boost payouts.

Mitigation Strategies:
✔ Hedge currency exposure via ETFs or forex tools.
✔ Invest in multinationals that earn revenue in USD.
✔ Diversify across multiple currencies.

When you invest internationally, you're not just betting on the company—you're also betting on their **local currency** vs. the U.S. dollar.

🔄 Currency Impact Example:

- You own a European stock that yields 5%.
- Euro weakens by 10% vs. USD.
- Your real yield = **5% - 10% = -5% (loss)**

📌 Pro Tip

Diversify across regions to reduce currency correlation. Use hedged ETFs for lower volatility.

10.3 Withholding Tax by Country

Many countries impose a withholding tax on dividends paid to foreign investors. Key rates:

•UK: 0% (for U.S. investors due to tax treaty)
•Canada: 15-25% (15% with U.S. treaty)
•France/Germany: 26.375%-30% (reduced to 15% with U.S. treaty)
•Australia: 30% (15% with U.S. treaty)
•Japan: 20.42% (10% with U.S. treaty)
How to Reclaim Taxes:
✔ Hold foreign stocks in a retirement account

(IRA/401k) where possible (some treaties exempt withholding taxes).
✔ File for a foreign tax credit (Form 1116) if held in a taxable account.

Many foreign governments **withhold a portion of your dividend at the source**—before it even hits your account.

Country	Default Withholding	U.S. Tax Treaty?	Claim Credit in Taxable?
Canada	15%	Yes	Yes (Form 1116)
Switzerland	35%	Yes	Partial credit
Australia	30%	Yes	Partial credit
U.K.	0% (for U.S. investors)	Yes	N/A

📌 **IRAs don't qualify** for tax treaty credits, so hold these in taxable accounts if you want to reclaim the taxes.

10.4 Emerging Markets Dividend Picks

Emerging markets offer high yields but come with higher risks:

•Brazil: Petrobras (PBR), Vale (VALE)
•China: China Mobile (CHL), Alibaba (BABA) – though dividends are inconsistent
•South Africa: Naspers (NPSNY), Sasol (SSL)
•India: Infosys (INFY), HDFC Bank (HDB)
Risks to Watch:
✔ Political instability

✔ Currency devaluations
✔ Lower dividend sustainability

American Depositary Receipts (ADRs) are a way to hold foreign stocks in your U.S. brokerage.

☑ **Benefits:**

- Priced in USD
- Traded on U.S. exchanges (easy to buy/sell)
- Often **include foreign tax details** on your 1099-DIV

| □ Tip: Look for Level I or Level II ADRs from major brokers —they simplify tax and reporting headaches. |

10.5 ADRs and International Dividends

Many foreign companies trade in the U.S. as American Depositary Receipts (ADRs), simplifying investment but with nuances:

•Sponsored vs. Unsponsored ADRs: Sponsored ADRs (e.g., TSM) have better regulatory compliance.
•Dividend Payments: ADRs pay dividends in USD, but banks may deduct small fees.
•Tax Treatment: Same withholding taxes apply unless held in a tax-advantaged account.

Key Takeaways:

☑ Diversify across stable, high-quality international dividend payers.

✅ Understand withholding taxes and optimize accounts to minimize them.

✅ Monitor currency risks and geopolitical factors in emerging markets.

✅ Prefer ADRs for ease of trading but check for fees and tax implications.

These ETFs give you exposure to international dividend payers without picking individual stocks.

ETF	Provider	Focus	Yield	Withholding Risk
VYMI	Vanguard	Developed + Emerging markets	~4.2 %	Moderate
IDV	iShares	High-yield developed markets	~5.1 %	Higher
PID	Invesco	Dividend achievers (global)	~3.5 %	Moderate
DWX	SPDR	High-dividend global stocks	~5.4 %	High

✅ Use ETFs to **spread currency, political, and sector risks** across countries.

🚨 Summary: What Global Dividend Investors Get Wrong

Myth	Reality
"Foreign stocks pay better dividends."	Not if currency drops or withholding taxes aren't recovered
"I'll just hold global ETFs in my IRA."	You'll lose withholding tax credits—use taxable accounts

Myth	Reality
"ADRs avoid all foreign tax problems."	ADRs **simplify**, but don't always eliminate the tax impact

Bottom Line

Going global opens up **higher yields**, **sector diversification**, and **economic insulation**—but you've got to account for currency moves, foreign taxes, and where you hold your assets.

> **Done right, international dividend investing expands your income empire—and reduces U.S.-centric risk.**

By carefully selecting international dividend stocks and managing risks, investors can enhance yield and global diversification.

Hidden Gems & Pitfalls in International Dividend Investing

Most investors focus on high yields when picking international dividend stocks, but the real game is in tax efficiency, currency dynamics, and structural risks—areas where even seasoned investors make costly mistakes.

The Overlooked Angle: "The Bermuda Tax Trick"

(How Some Companies Avoid Withholding Taxes)

What Most Investors Miss:
Many multinationals legally route dividends through tax-friendly jurisdictions (e.g., Bermuda, Ireland, Netherlands) to reduce withholding taxes for shareholders.

•Example:

•British American Tobacco (BTI) is UK-based but incorporated in British Bermuda—meaning no UK withholding tax (vs. 15% for other UK stocks).
•Shell (SHEL) moved its tax residency to the UK but retains Dutch/Irish structures for tax efficiency.

Pro-Tip:
✔ Check the country of incorporation (not just HQ) in SEC filings—some stocks have lower or zero withholding taxes due to legal structuring.

💡 *Pro-Tips & Hidden Pitfalls*

1. The "ADR Fee" Scam (That No One Talks About)

•Many ADRs charge hidden custody fees (0.01%–0.05% per dividend).
•Example: If you own Siemens (SIEGY), BNY Mellon deducts a small fee before paying you.
✔ Fix: Buy the local shares via a broker like Interactive Brokers if fees outweigh benefits.

2. Emerging Market Dividends Are a Trap (Sometimes)

•High yields in Brazil, Russia, or Turkey often come with currency crashes.
•Example: Petrobras (PBR) had a 20%+ yield in 2021… but the Brazilian Real fell 40% vs. USD in 5 years, wiping out gains.

✔ Fix: Only invest in EM dividends if the company earns in USD/EUR (e.g., Vale (VALE) sells iron ore in USD).

3. The "Euro Dividend Trap" (Why European Stocks Aren't as Safe as You Think)

•Many EU companies pay high yields but don't grow dividends (e.g., telecoms like Vodafone).
•Example: Telefónica (TEF) cut its dividend 3 times since 2010 despite a tempting yield.
✔ Fix: Focus on global consumer giants (Unilever, Nestlé) over local EU utilities/telcos.

4. The Retirement Account Loophole (Avoid Withholding Tax Legally)

•Most investors don't know that holding foreign stocks in an IRA/401(k) can bypass withholding taxes in some cases.
•Example: Canadian stocks (like TD Bank) normally withhold 15%, but in an IRA, it's 0% due to US-Canada tax treaties.
✔ Fix: Use retirement accounts for high-withholding-tax stocks (Canada, France, Germany).

🎯 *Final Takeaways: How to Win at International Dividends*

✅ Tax Hack: Favor stocks incorporated in Bermuda, Ireland, Netherlands for lower/no withholding taxes.
✅ ADR Trap: Watch for hidden fees—sometimes local shares are better.
✅ EM Warning: Avoid high yields in weak currencies unless

the company earns in USD.

✅ Euro Caution: EU dividends look safe but often stagnate or get cut—prioritize global brands.

✅ Retirement Trick: Hold high-tax foreign stocks in an IRA/401(k) to legally dodge withholding taxes.

By mastering these **hidden rules**, you can boost net dividend income while avoiding costly mistakes most investors make.

Chapter 10: Monthly Dividend Stocks

Monthly dividend stocks attract income-focused investors with their predictable cash flow, but they come with unique risks and opportunities. This chapter breaks down the best strategies for investing in monthly payers—and the pitfalls to avoid.

"Turn Your Portfolio Into a Monthly Paycheck with These Consistent Payers"

Quarterly payouts are fine—but monthly dividends? That's **real cash-flow freedom**. Monthly dividend stocks are ideal for investors who want consistent income to match their living expenses, bills, or reinvestment goals.

📌 *11.1 Top Monthly Dividend Stocks*

Not all monthly dividend stocks are equal. Here are the highest-quality options across sectors:

◈ *Blue-Chip Monthly Payers*

•Realty Income (O) – "The Monthly Dividend Company," a stalwart REIT with 640+ consecutive monthly payments.
•Main Street Capital (MAIN) – A top-tier BDC with a strong track record.
•EPR Properties (EPR) – Specialty REIT focused on experiential real estate (movie theaters, ski resorts).

◈ *High-Yield but Higher Risk*

•AGNC Investment Corp (AGNC) – Mortgage REIT with ~14% yield, but sensitive to interest rates.
•Gladstone Commercial (GOOD) – Industrial/office REIT with ~9% yield, but higher leverage risk.
Pro Tip:
✔ Focus on dividend sustainability (payout ratio, FFO coverage) over yield alone.

These are the most popular and consistent monthly payers right now:

Ticker	Company Name	Sector	Dividend Yield	Notes
O	Realty Income	REIT - Retail	~5.0%	The "Monthly Dividend Company"
STAG	STAG Industrial	REIT - Industrial	~4.2%	Focused on e-commerce warehouses
EPR	EPR Properties	REIT - Entertainme nt	~7.5%	Movie theaters, attractions
MAIN	Main Street Capital	BDC	~6.5%	High-quality business development
SLG.PJ	SL Green Realty (Preferred)	REIT - Office	~8.0%	Preferred shares, fixed income feel

📌 **These stocks pay 12 times per year**, making them perfect for retirement income or monthly reinvestment schedules.

🔄 *11.2 Monthly Dividends vs. Quarterly*

Pros of Monthly Dividends:

✅ Smoother cash flow – Better for budgeting, especially for retirees.
✅ Compounding advantage – Reinvesting more frequently can slightly boost long-term returns.
✅ Psychological benefit – Regular payouts can reduce emotional investing mistakes.

Cons of Monthly Dividends:

❌ Often higher risk – Many monthly payers are REITs, BDCs, or high-yield traps.
❌ Lower growth – Most don't increase payouts as aggressively as quarterly dividend aristocrats.

Pro Tip:
✔ Blend monthly payers (for cash flow) + quarterly growers (for long-term upside) in your portfolio.

Aspect	Monthly Dividends	Quarterly Dividends
Frequency	12 times/year	4 times/year
Income Consistency	High	Moderate
Budgeting Alignment	Monthly bills	Harder to match expenses
Compound Frequency	Higher	Lower
Payer Pool Size	Limited	Vast

💡 *Pro Tip:*

> If you live off dividends, monthly payers make **budgeting easier** and reduce **cash-flow volatility**.

🏢 *11.3 Best Monthly Dividend REITs*

REITs dominate the monthly dividend space. The best ones balance yield, growth, and safety:

REIT	Yield	Sector	Risk Level
Realty Income (O)	5.5%	Retail/ Commercial	Low
STAG Industrial (STAG)	4.1%	Industrial Warehouses	Medium
Agree Realty (ADC)	4.8%	Net-Lease Retail	Low-Medium
LTC Properties (LTC)	6.3%	Healthcare (Senior	Medium-High

REIT	Yield	Sector	Risk Level
		Housing)	

Hidden Pitfall:

⚠ Interest rate sensitivity – Rising rates hurt REITs by increasing borrowing costs.

Pro Tip:

✔ Prefer net-lease REITs (O, ADC) over mortgage REITs (AGNC, NLY) for lower volatility.

Retirement income: Aligns with monthly bills (mortgage, utilities, food)

- **DRIP investing**: More compounding frequency = faster share accumulation
- **Passive income goals**: Feels like a "paycheck from your portfolio"

⚠ Watch Out:

Some monthly dividend payers offer **high yield but low quality**. Always check payout ratio, cash flow, and business model.

11.4 Calendar Planning with Monthly Payers

Smart investors stagger payouts to ensure weekly or bi-weekly income:

Example Portfolio with 12+ Payouts/Month:

Stock	Payout Date	Yield
Realty Income (O)	15th of month	5.5%
Shaw Communications	1st of month	6.2%

Stock	Payout Date	Yield
(SJR)		
Pembina Pipeline (PBA)	15th of month	5.8%
Gladstone Land (LAND)	End of month	3.4%

Pro Tip:
✔ Use a dividend calendar tool (like Dividend.com) to optimize cash flow timing.

Want monthly income **and** diversification? Use these ETFs:

ETF	Provider	Yield	Strategy
JEPI	JPMorgan	~7.0%	Covered call + equity blend
QYLD	Global X	~12.0%	NASDAQ 100 + monthly options income
HYMB	SPDR	~4.5%	High-yield muni bonds (tax-advantaged)
PFF	iShares	~6.2%	Preferred stock income

📌 These are ideal for those wanting monthly income with **built-in diversification**.

⚠ *11.5 Risk Profile of Monthly Stocks*

Many monthly dividend stocks are riskier than they appear:

Biggest Risks:

1.High Leverage (REITs/BDCs) – Many rely on debt, making them vulnerable in downturns.

2. Yield Traps – Some sustain payouts by diluting shareholders (e.g., AGNC).
3. Interest Rate Sensitivity – REITs and BDCs underperform when rates rise.

How to Mitigate Risk:

✔ Diversify across sectors (REITs, BDCs, utilities, pipelines).
✔ Avoid ultra-high yields (>10%) unless you understand the business model.
✔ Monitor payout ratios (REITs: check FFO payout ratio; BDCs: look at NII coverage).

Myth	Reality
"Monthly payers are safer."	Not always—some use leverage or risky business models.
"More payments = more return."	True **only if dividends are safe and growing.**
"I can live off monthly dividends alone."	Possible, but takes capital and careful planning.

□ *Pro Tips:*

- Track income with a **dividend calendar**.
- Use **dividend laddering** (different stocks pay at different times) to smooth flow.
- Check for **dividend stability**, not just frequency.

🚦 Bottom Line

Monthly dividend stocks give your portfolio a **paycheck-like rhythm**, making them perfect for predictable income. But don't get blinded by yield—make sure the business is **solid, sustainable, and shareholder-friendly**.

> Use them strategically to build a portfolio that pays you like a job—**without ever clocking in.**

🎯 Final Takeaways: How to Invest Wisely in Monthly Dividend Stocks

✅ Best Picks: Stick to high-quality REITs (O, STAG, ADC) and low-debt BDCs (MAIN).
✅ Avoid Yield Traps: Anything yielding >10% likely has unsustainable payouts.
✅ Optimize Cash Flow: Stagger payouts for consistent monthly income.
✅ Watch Interest Rates: REITs struggle when rates rise—adjust allocations accordingly.

By balancing **yield, safety, and cash flow timing**, you can build a **reliable monthly income portfolio** without falling into high-risk traps. 🚀

The Hidden Truth About Monthly Dividend Stocks (What Nobody Tells You)

Most investors chase monthly dividends for the **psychological comfort of frequent payouts**, but there's a **dark side**—and a few **exploitable advantages**—that most people completely miss.

🔥 The Big Myth: "Monthly Dividends Compound Faster" (Spoiler: They Don't)

What People Get Wrong:

Many investors believe **monthly dividends automatically grow wealth faster** due to more frequent compounding.
Reality Check:

- If a stock pays **3% annually**, it doesn't matter if it's paid **monthly (0.25% per month) or quarterly (0.75% per quarter)**—the end result is the same.
- **Compounding only works if you reinvest**, and most brokers don't support fractional shares for small monthly payouts.

Pro-Tip:
✔ If you're **not reinvesting**, monthly vs. quarterly makes **no mathematical difference**—focus on **total yield and growth** instead.

💡 The "Paycheck Illusion" (Why Monthly Dividends Feel Safer Than They Are)

Psychological Trap:

- Investors **mistake frequency for safety**—just because a stock pays every month doesn't mean it's low-risk.
- **Example: AGNC (14% yield)** pays monthly but has **eroded capital by -50%+ since 2010**.

Pro-Tip:
✔ Judge stocks by **payout sustainability (FFO coverage, debt levels)**, not payout frequency.

🎯 The Best (and Worst) Ways to Use Monthly Dividends

✅ Smart Use-Case: Retirement Cash Flow

- If you depend on dividends for living expenses, **monthly payers smooth out cash flow**.
- **Example:** Holding **O, MAIN, and STAG** can provide **12+ paychecks a year** without selling shares.

❌ Dumb Use-Case: Chasing Yield Without Due Diligence

- **Example: Orchid Island Capital (ORC)** pays **16% monthly** but has **slashed dividends 5+ times** and diluted shareholders.
- **Pro-Tip:**
  ✔ Best Monthly Dividend Stocks = Low debt + growing AFFO (for REITs) or NII (for BDCs).

⚠ Hidden Pitfalls of Monthly Dividend Stocks

1. The "Dividend Cut Domino Effect"

- Many monthly payers are **REITs or BDCs**, which **must distribute 90% of income**—leaving little room for error.
- **Example: Global Net Lease (GNL)** cut its monthly dividend in 2023 due to rising interest costs.

  How to Spot Trouble Early:
  ✔ Watch **FFO (Funds From Operations) trends**—declining FFO = dividend cut risk.

2. The "Silent Killer" – Fee Drag in BDCs & Mortgage REITs

- **BDCs (like MAIN) and mREITs (like AGNC) charge high management fees** that eat into returns.
- **Example:** Some BDCs take **20% of profits** (2% management fee + 20% incentive fee).

Pro-Tip:

✔ Check the **fee structure** before buying—lower-fee BDCs (like **ARCC**) perform better long-term.

3. The "Liquidity Trap" – Low Volume, High Spreads

- Many monthly payers are **small-cap stocks with thin trading volume**, leading to:
  - **Wide bid-ask spreads** (costing you 1-2% on entry/exit).
  - **Flash crashes** (e.g., **GLAD dropped 30% in minutes** due to illiquidity).

Fix:

✔ Stick to **liquid monthly payers (O, STAG, ADC)** to avoid slippage.

🚀 Pro-Tips for Monthly Dividend Masters

✔ **Blend Monthly + Quarterly Stocks** – Best of both worlds (cash flow + growth).

✔ **Auto-Reinvest? Go Quarterly** – Fewer, larger payouts = better compounding with fractional shares.

✔ **Use a "Dividend Calendar"** – Stagger payouts for **weekly**

income (e.g., O on the 15th + GOOD at month-end).
✔ **Avoid >8% Yields** – Most are **yield traps** with dividend cuts looming.

Final Thought:

Monthly dividends are **great for cash flow** but **terrible if picked blindly**. Focus on **business quality**, not frequency! 🎯

Chapter 11: Sector Analysis for Dividends

Dividend investing varies **wildly** by sector—some industries are **cash cows**, while others are **dividend traps in disguise**. This chapter reveals the **best dividend sectors**, hidden risks, and **pro strategies** to maximize income.

"Not All Sectors Pay Equally—Here's Where the Real Dividend Power Lies"

A smart dividend investor doesn't just pick stocks—they pick **sectors strategically**. Some industries are income machines. Others are dividend disasters in disguise. Knowing the difference can mean the difference between consistent income and a payout cut.

⚡ 12.1 Utilities with Strong Dividends

The Safe Haven (But With Hidden Risks)

Utilities are **classic dividend stocks**—regulated cash flows, high yields, and recession resistance. But **rising interest rates** have crushed them recently.

◈ Top Utility Dividend Stocks

Stock	Yield	Dividend Growth Streak	Risk Factor
NextEra Energy (NEE)	3.1%	28+ years	High valuation
Duke Energy (DUK)	4.2%	18+ years	Debt exposure
Southern Company (SO)	4.0%	22+ years	Nuclear project risks

⚠ *Hidden Pitfalls*

- **Interest rate sensitivity** – Utilities are **bond proxies**, so they fall when rates rise.
- **Regulatory risk** – Governments can cap profits (see **UK windfall taxes**).
- **Debt levels** – Many utilities carry **heavy debt (60-70%+ debt-to-equity)**.

Pro-Tip:
✔ Buy utilities **after Fed rate cuts** (they rally hard).
✔ Prefer **regulated utilities (DUK, SO)** over merchant power plants (less volatility).

◈ **Overview:**
Utilities are known for **stable cash flow** and **regulated pricing**, making them a favorite among conservative dividend investors.

Top Picks	Yield	Notes
Duke Energy (DUK)	~4.1 %	Electric utility, consistent growth
NextEra Energy (NEE)	~2.6 %	Focus on clean energy + dividend growth
Dominion Energy (D)	~5.3 %	Reliable but with occasional payout stress

📌 *Utilities are defensive—often perform well in recessions.*

💰 12.2 Financial Sector Dividend Trends

Banks vs. Insurance vs. Asset Managers

Financials are **dividend rebounders** after the 2008 crisis and COVID cuts.

◈ **Best Financial Dividend Stocks**

Category	Stock	Yield	Key Metric
Big Banks	JPMorgan (JPM)	2.4%	CET1 Ratio >13%
Insurance	Chubb (CB)	1.4%	Underwriting profit
Asset Mgmt	BlackRock (BLK)	2.5%	AUM growth

⚠ ***Hidden Risks***

- **Yield traps** – Some European banks (e.g., **Credit Suisse**) had high yields before collapsing.
- **Economic sensitivity** – Banks cut dividends in recessions (see **2020 COVID suspensions**).

Pro-Tip:

✔ Focus on **banks with strong CET1 ratios (>12%)**— they're safer in downturns.

✔ **Insurance stocks (CB, TRV)** are more stable than banks.

◈ **Overview:**

Banks and financials tend to pay good dividends when rates are rising and the economy is growing.

Top Picks	Yield	Notes
JPMorgan Chase (JPM)	~3.2 %	Strong balance sheet, consistent growth
Bank of Montreal (BMO)	~5.0 %	Canadian bank, international exposure
Aflac (AFL)	~2.5 %	Insurer with growing dividend track record

📌 *Watch for cyclical risks—banks often cut dividends in crises.*

🪙 12.3 Energy Stocks with High Yields

The Boom/Bust Cycle (How to Play It Right)

Energy dividends are **huge but volatile**—oil prices dictate payouts.

◈ **Best Energy Dividend Plays**

Type	Stock	Yield	Payout Safety
Integrated	Exxon (XOM)	3.3%	Very safe (50% payout ratio)
Midstream	Enterprise (EPD)	7.2%	Rock-solid (DCF-covered)
High-Yield	Energy Transfer (ET)	8.0%	Growing but higher risk

⚠ ***Hidden Pitfalls***

- **Commodity risk** – Oil crashes = dividend cuts (see **2020 carnage**).
- **MLP tax complexity** – K-1 forms (annoying for taxable accounts).

Pro-Tip:
✔ **Midstream (pipelines) > E&P** – Less volatile, fees-based revenue.
✔ Buy **after oil crashes** (best yields appear when fear is high).

12.3 🛢 Energy Stocks with High Yields

◈ ***Overview:***

Energy stocks can offer **high payouts**, but they're notoriously cyclical and sensitive to commodity prices.

Top Picks	Yield	Notes
ExxonMobil (XOM)	~3.7 %	Strong legacy dividend player
Chevron (CVX)	~4.0 %	Integrated energy, reliable dividends
Enbridge (ENB)	~7.3 %	Canadian pipeline giant (midstream)

⚠ *Yields may look great—but energy downturns can wreck income flow.*

📡 12.4 Telecom Dividend Players

The Good, The Bad, and The Ugly

Telecoms offer **high yields but low growth**—some are **dividend traps**.

◈ Top Telecom Dividends

Stock	Yield	Dividend Safety
Verizon (VZ)	6.5%	Shaky (high debt)
AT&T (T)	6.7%	Post-cut, now safer
BCE (BCE)	7.1%	Stable (Canadian telecom)

⚠ *Hidden Risks*

- **Debt bombs** – Verizon (150B+) are **leveraged**.
- **Technological disruption** – 5G capex is crushing cash flows.

Pro-Tip:

✔ Prefer **Canadian telecoms (BCE, TU)** – Lower debt, regulated markets.

✔ Avoid **T and VZ** if rates keep rising (debt refinancing hurts).

◈ Overview:

Telecoms offer decent dividends due to stable recurring revenue —but beware of heavy debt and low growth.

Top Picks	Yield	Notes
Verizon (VZ)	~6.7 %	High yield, but declining revenues

Top Picks	Yield	Notes
AT&T (T)	~7.0 %	Restructuring; dividend risk remains
BCE Inc. (BCE)	~6.1 %	Canadian telecom with stability

📌 *Great income now, but limited long-term growth—treat as income anchors, not growth assets.*

💻 12.5 Tech Stocks That Pay Dividends

The New Dividend Kings (Yes, Tech!)

Tech was once **growth-only**, but now **mature giants** pay growing dividends.

◈ Best Tech Dividend Stocks

Stock	Yield	Dividend Growth	Cash Cow Business
Apple (AAPL)	0.6%	11+ years	iPhone + Services
Microsoft (MSFT)	0.7%	20+ years	Azure + Office
Broadcom (AVGO)	1.9%	12+ years	Semiconductors + Software

⚠ ***Hidden Risks***

- **Low yields** – Don’t expect 4%+ from tech (yet).
- **Growth slowdown risk** – If innovation stalls, dividends could stagnate.

Pro-Tip:
✔ **Focus on dividend growth** – AAPL & MSFT double payouts every ~5 years.
✔ **Wait for pullbacks** – Tech dividends are better when bought at fair valuations.

◈ Overview:

Tech isn't traditionally a dividend sector—but a few mature players pay reliable, growing dividends.

Top Picks	Yield	Notes
Microsoft (MSFT)	~0.8 %	Low yield, high growth
Apple (AAPL)	~0.6 %	Fast-growing dividend, massive cash flow
Broadcom (AVGO)	~2.0 %	Strong growth + serious payout

📌 *Dividend tech = capital growth + future dividend increases —best for long-term compounding.*

□ Sector Allocation Pro Tips

Tip	Why It Matters
Don't overload REITs or energy	High yield ≠ stability. Overexposure = high risk.
Mix growth & yield sectors	Blend tech/healthcare (growth) with utilities/REITs (income).
Rebalance annually	Yields and sectors shift—adjust to stay balanced.

🚨 Summary: What Most People Get Wrong

Myth	Reality
"All high-yield sectors are safe."	High yield often means high risk—look deeper.
"Tech doesn't pay dividends."	Some tech giants pay—and grow them aggressively.
"Financials always pay."	Many cut dividends during 2008 and other downturns.

🚦 Bottom Line

The sector you invest in determines **how consistent, safe, and scalable** your dividend income will be. Build a **sector-diversified income engine**, and your portfolio can keep paying no matter what the economy throws at you.

🎯 Final Takeaways: How to Dominate Sector-Based Dividend Investing

✅ **Utilities** – Buy **after rate cuts**, avoid overleveraged players.

✅ **Financials** – Stick to **strong banks (JPM) and insurers (CB)**.

✅ **Energy** – **Midstream (EPD) > E&P**, buy when oil is hated.

✅ **Telecom** – **Canada (BCE) > US (VZ, T)** due to lower debt.

✅ **Tech** – **AAPL, MSFT, AVGO** are future dividend aristocrats.

Biggest Mistake to Avoid:

❌ **Chasing yield without checking debt & payout safety.**

By **picking the right sectors at the right time**, you can build a **high-income, low-risk** dividend portfolio. 🚀

□ Sector Allocation Pro Tips

Tip	Why It Matters
Don't overload REITs or energy	High yield ≠ stability. Overexposure = high risk.
Mix growth & yield sectors	Blend tech/healthcare (growth) with utilities/REITs (income).
Rebalance annually	Yields and sectors shift—adjust to stay balanced.

🚨 Summary: What Most People Get Wrong

Myth	Reality
"All high-yield sectors are safe."	High yield often means high risk—look deeper.
"Tech doesn't pay dividends."	Some tech giants pay—and grow them aggressively.
"Financials always pay."	Many cut dividends during 2008 and other downturns.

🚦 Bottom Line

The sector you invest in determines **how consistent, safe, and scalable** your dividend income will be. Build a **sector-**

diversified income engine, and your portfolio can keep paying no matter what the economy throws at you.

Chapter 12: Dividend Investing for Retirement

Retirement investing isn't just about total returns—it's about predictable income, capital preservation, and sleep-well-at-night stability. Dividend investing is uniquely suited for retirees, but most people make critical mistakes that jeopardize their golden years.

"Turn Your Portfolio Into a Lifetime Income Machine"

Retirement isn't about chasing yield—it's about **preserving wealth while generating enough cash flow** to cover expenses. Done right, dividend investing can provide stable, inflation-resistant income that lasts decades.

🔥 *14.1 Building Retirement Income with Dividends*

The #1 Mistake Retirees Make:

They chase high yields (6%+) without considering sustainability, exposing themselves to dividend cuts and capital erosion.

The Right Approach:

A three-bucket strategy for retirement income:

Bucket	Purpose	Example Holdings
Safety Bucket (40%)	Preserve capital, steady income	**JNJ, PG, PEP, SO**

Bucket	**Purpose**	**Example Holdings**
Growth Bucket (30%)	Inflation-beating dividend growth	**AAPL, MSFT, AVGO**
Yield Bucket (30%)	Higher income (but still safe)	**O, EPD, MAIN**

Pro-Tip:
✔ Never rely solely on dividends—keep 1-2 years of cash to avoid selling in downturns.

Goal: Generate monthly income that covers basic living expenses

To do this, you need:

- A diversified portfolio across dividend sectors
- A mix of **growth + yield** to combat inflation
- Safe, tax-efficient income streams

Example Target:

- $40,000/year in retirement income
- 4% dividend yield → You need ~$1 million invested in dividend-paying assets

📌 **Pro Tip:**

Build an **income ladder**: Monthly-paying REITs + quarterly blue chips staggered across different months for consistent cash flow.

🛡 *14.2 Safe Dividend Stocks for Retirees*

The "Widow & Orphan" Test:

Would this stock still pay dividends in a recession, market crash, or inflation spike?

Top 5 Safest Dividend Stocks for Retirees:

1.Johnson & Johnson (JNJ) – 60+ years of dividend growth, healthcare resilience.
2.Procter & Gamble (PG) – 68+ years of hikes, recession-proof products.
3.PepsiCo (PEP) – 50+ years of growth, snacks + beverages = stability.
4.Realty Income (O) – 640+ consecutive monthly dividends, fortress balance sheet.
5.NextEra Energy (NEE) – Leading utility with renewable growth.

Hidden Risk:
⚠ Even "safe" stocks can fall 20-30% in a bear market—diversify across sectors.

Pro-Tip:
✔ Avoid stocks with >65% payout ratios—they're vulnerable in downturns.

These stocks have long track records, low payout ratios, and stable cash flow—ideal for retirees.

Ticker	Company	Yield	Why It's Safe
JNJ	Johnson & Johnson	~2.9%	Dividend King, recession-resistant sector
PG	Procter & Gamble	~2.4%	Consumer staples, reliable cash flow
O	Realty Income	~5.0%	Monthly income, diversified REIT
SCHD	Schwab Dividend ETF	~3.6%	Quality filter, built-in diversification
WEC	WEC Energy Group	~3.7%	Utility with low volatility

📌 *These aren't just about yield—they're about protecting capital too.*

📉 *14.3 Role of Dividends in Withdrawal Strategy*

The 4% Rule vs. Dividend Income Strategy

•Traditional 4% Rule: Sell 4% of portfolio yearly (but selling in downturns destroys capital).
•Dividend Strategy: Live off dividends only (no selling required).
Problem:
Most retirees can't live off dividends alone unless they have $1M+ invested.

Solution:
✔ Hybrid Approach – Cover 50-70% of expenses with dividends, sell 3% max in bad years.

Pro-Tip:

✔ Target a 3.5-4.5% portfolio yield—higher is usually too risky.

Dividends can **supplement or fully fund** your retirement withdrawals, reducing the need to sell shares.

☑ **Common Models:**

- **Yield Shield Strategy**: Live entirely off dividends
- **Partial Withdrawal**: Use dividends + some capital gains
- **Bucket Strategy**: High-yield assets in short-term bucket, growth assets in long-term

| 🔧 Tool: Use portfolio simulators like Portfolio Visualizer to test how much income your portfolio can sustainably produce. |

⚠ *14.4 Managing Risk in Retirement*

The 3 Biggest Risks for Retired Dividend Investors:

1.Sequence of Returns Risk – A market crash early in retirement can ruin you.

•Fix: Keep 2 years of cash to avoid selling low.

2.Inflation Risk – Fixed incomes lose buying power over time.

•Fix: Hold dividend growers (AAPL, HD, LOW).

3.Dividend Cut Risk – One bad cut can wreck your income.

•Fix: Diversify across 30+ stocks (no single stock >3% of portfolio).

•

Pro-Tip:

✔ Rebalance annually—sell winners, buy undervalued dividend payers.

Common Retirement Risks:

Risk	How Dividends Help
Market volatility	Steady income even if prices drop
Inflation	Dividend growers can beat rising costs
Sequence of returns	Dividends reduce need to sell shares
Longevity	Dividend compounding supports long-term income

📌 **Pro Tip:**

Avoid overconcentration in one sector (e.g., REITs). Diversification is key for sustainable payouts.

📊 *14.5 Case Studies of Retired Dividend Investors*

Case Study #1: The "High-Yield Disaster"

•Portfolio: 100% in AGNC, ORC, and other 10%+ yielders.
•Result: Dividend cuts led to 50% income loss + capital depletion.
•Lesson: Yield is meaningless if unsustainable.

Case Study #2: The "Dividend Growth Millionaire"

•Portfolio: 50% low-yield growers (MSFT, HD), 50% steady payers (JNJ, O).
•Result: Income doubled in 10 years while capital grew.

•Lesson: Dividend growth beats high yield long-term.

Case Study #3: The "Cash Buffer Genius"

•Strategy: Held 2 years of expenses in cash, only sold stocks in up years.
•Result: Survived 2008 and 2020 crashes without panic-selling.
•Lesson: Liquidity = survival.

□ **Martha, 68** — $900,000 portfolio

- 70% dividend stocks, 30% fixed income
- Focus on monthly payers (O, MAIN, JEPI)
- Income: ~$35,000/year in dividends
- Reinvests 20% to offset inflation

🧓 **James, 62 — FIRE (Financial Independence Retire Early)**

- $1.2M portfolio
- Mix of SCHD, individual dividend stocks, and international ETFs
- Lives on ~3.5% withdrawal rate, using dividends as first layer
- Taps Roth conversions strategically for tax efficiency

🚦 **Bottom Line**

Dividend investing in retirement isn't just about income—it's about **stability, predictability, and sustainability**. With the right structure, you can enjoy your golden years without worrying about selling during bear markets or running out of money.

> "The best retirement portfolios are boring, diversified, and pay you every month."

🎯 Final Retirement Dividend Blueprint

✅ Safety First – Stick to dividend kings/aristocrats (JNJ, PG, KO).
✅ Growth Matters – Allocate 30% to dividend growers (AAPL, MSFT).
✅ Cash Buffer – Keep 1-2 years of expenses in cash/CDs.
✅ Diversify – No single stock >3%, no sector >20%.
✅ Hybrid Withdrawal – Cover 70% with dividends, sell 3% max in bad years.

Biggest Mistake to Avoid:
❌ Reaching for yield instead of safety.

By following this plan, you can **turn your portfolio into a paycheck** that lasts **30+ years**.

Chapter 13: Risks in Dividend Investing –

The Hidden Dangers Every Investor Must Know

Dividend investing is often seen as a safe strategy, but it comes with unique risks that can destroy income streams and erode capital. Many investors learn these lessons the hard way. This chapter reveals the biggest threats to dividend portfolios and how to avoid them.

⚠ *"Dividends Aren't Guaranteed—Here's How to Protect Your Passive Income"*

Dividend investing is often seen as "safe"—but that's only true if you understand the risks. From cuts and economic shocks to rising interest rates, dividends come with their own landmines. Here's how to spot them before they explode.

⚠ *16.1 Dividend Cuts and Suspensions*

The Silent Killer of Income Portfolios

Nothing hurts more than a dividend cut—it slashes your income and crushes the stock price.

Top 5 Warning Signs of a Coming Dividend Cut:

1.Payout Ratio > 90% (Unless it's a REIT/MLP)
2.Rising Debt / Declining Cash Flow
3.Sector-Wide Downturn (E.g., oil crash, banking crisis)
4.Management Hints at "Reviewing Capital Allocation"

5.Stock Price Collapse (Market often knows before the announcement)
Recent Examples of Painful Cuts:

•AT&T (T) – Cut dividend -50% in 2022 after Warner Bros. spin-off.
•General Electric (GE) – Slashed payout -90% in 2018 amid financial troubles.
•Occidental Petroleum (OXY) – Cut -86% in 2020 when oil crashed.
Pro-Tip:
✔ Check dividend safety metrics (payout ratio, free cash flow coverage) before buying.
✔ Diversify across sectors so one cut doesn't wreck your income.

🚨 *The #1 Risk in Dividend Investing*

Companies can reduce or stop dividends anytime—especially in downturns.

Common Causes of Dividend Cuts

Falling earnings

High debt or unsustainable payout ratio

Recession or sector collapse

Shift in capital allocation strategy

Recent Examples:

- **AT&T (T)** cut its dividend in 2022 after spinoffs

- **Disney (DIS)** suspended its dividend during COVID
- **Boeing (BA)** eliminated its dividend after cash flow dried up

📌 **Pro Tip:**

Avoid companies with payout ratios over 80% or negative free cash flow. These are warning signs.

📉 *16.2 Sector-Specific Risks*

Not All Dividends Are Created Equal

Some sectors are far riskier than others.

Sector	Biggest Risk	Example Stocks
Energy	Oil price crashes	OXY, CVX
REITs	Rising interest rates	O, WPC
Banks	Loan defaults, rate squeezes	JPM, BAC
Telecom	Massive debt loads	VZ, T
Utilities	Regulatory risk, high debt	DUK, SO

Pro-Tip:

✔ Limit exposure to any single sector (max 20% of portfolio).
✔ Prefer sectors with pricing power (consumer staples, healthcare).

Not all sectors carry the same dividend risk:

Sector	Dividend Risk	Comment
Utilities	□ Low	Stable cash flow, regulated returns
REITs	□ Moderate	High payout mandates, sensitive to economy
Energy	● High	Commodity-driven, cyclical
Financials	□ Moderate	Sensitive to interest rates & credit cycles
Tech	□ Low	If they pay, it's usually sustainable
Telecom	● High	Capital-intensive, shrinking revenue risks

⚠ **Watch Out:**

High yield in a risky sector = likely dividend cut during the next downturn.

📈 *16.3 Interest Rate Risk and Dividends*

Why Rising Rates Crush Dividend Stocks

•Bonds become more attractive → Investors sell dividend stocks for higher yields.
•REITs & Utilities suffer most (they rely on debt financing).
Case Study: 2022 Bloodbath

•Realty Income (O) fell -30% as rates surged.
•Southern Company (SO) dropped -25%.
How to Protect Yourself:
✔ Shorten duration – Avoid long-duration dividend stocks (like utilities).
✔ Focus on companies with strong pricing power (e.g., PEP, KO).

Why Rates Matter:

When interest rates rise, dividend stocks often **underperform**:

- Bonds become more attractive → competition for yield
- REITs and utilities may decline due to rate-sensitive debt structures

What Happens:

- **REITs** and **bond-like equities** drop in price
- Cost of borrowing increases → cash flow squeezed

📌 **Tip:**

Focus on dividend growers with low debt when rates are rising (e.g., JNJ, PG, MSFT).

🧮 *16.4 Inflation Impact on Dividends*

The Silent Dividend Killer

Inflation erodes purchasing power, making flat dividends worthless over time.

Winners vs. Losers in High Inflation:

Winners (Dividends Grow Faster Than Inflation)	Losers (Dividends Don't Keep Up)
Consumer Staples (PG, KO)	Fixed-Income REITs (O, WPC)
Tech (AAPL, MSFT)	Telecom (VZ, T)

Winners (Dividends Grow Faster Than Inflation)	Losers (Dividends Don't Keep Up)
Industrial (HD, CAT)	Traditional Utilities (DUK, SO)

Pro-Tip:
✔ Prioritize dividend growers (5%+ annual hikes) over high-yield traps.

Inflation eats away at **purchasing power**. If your dividends don't grow, you fall behind.

Protection Against Inflation

Own dividend growth stocks (e.g., aristocrats)

Reinvest dividends to compound faster

Avoid fixed dividend payers (preferreds, bonds)

📌 Companies that raise dividends annually help keep up with the cost of living.

📊 *16.5 Managing Portfolio Volatility*

How to Sleep Well During Market Crashes

Dividend stocks aren't immune to volatility—many drop just as hard in bear markets.

5 Rules to Reduce Volatility:

1. Diversify Across Sectors (No more than 20% in any one industry).

2.Hold Some Low-Beta Stocks (e.g., PG, JNJ, KO).
3.Keep Cash for Buying Opportunities (Don't be forced to sell low).
4.Avoid Over-Leveraged Companies (Debt magnifies losses).
5.Use Covered Calls for Extra Income (Reduces downside risk).

Pro-Tip:
✔ Rebalance annually—trim winners, buy undervalued dividend payers.

Dividend stocks **aren't immune to market crashes**. In fact, high-yielders often fall harder.

How to Reduce Risk:

- Diversify across sectors and geographies
- Blend high yield (JEPI, O) with growth payers (MSFT, V, SCHD)
- Maintain a **cash buffer or bond allocation** for drawdowns
- Track beta: look for **low-volatility dividend ETFs** like SPLV or USMV

📌 **Pro Tip:**

Don't stretch for yield. A well-balanced 3.5–4.5% yielding portfolio with strong fundamentals is safer and more sustainable long term.

🚨 Summary: Key Dividend Risks

Risk	Avoidance Strategy
Dividend Cuts	Monitor payout ratio, earnings, debt
Sector Collapse	Diversify into multiple low-correlation sectors
Interest Rate Spike	Limit REITs, high-debt companies
Inflation	Choose companies with a track record of dividend growth
Market Volatility	Balance with low-beta stocks and ETFs

🚦 Bottom Line

Dividend investing works best when paired with **risk awareness and smart portfolio construction**. The key isn't just generating income—it's protecting it when the market turns against you.

> ***"Strong dividends come from strong businesses. Anything else is just yield bait."***

🎯 Final Checklist for Dividend Risk Management

- ✅ Avoid payout ratios > 90% (Unless REIT/MLP).
- ✅ Diversify across sectors (No more than 20% in one).
- ✅ Prepare for rising rates (Limit utility/REIT exposure).
- ✅ Focus on dividend growth (Beat inflation).
- ✅ Keep cash reserves (Avoid forced selling in crashes).

Biggest Mistake to Avoid:
❌ Assuming "high yield = safe." (Many high yielders are dividend traps.)

By following these rules, you can **protect your income** and **avoid catastrophic losses.** 🚀

Chapter 14: Case Studies of Dividend Investors – Real Stories, Real Lessons

Dividend investing looks simple—until you see real-world portfolios and the hard lessons investors learned along the way. This chapter dives into actual case studies, from early retirees to beginners who became experts, revealing what worked, what failed, and how you can avoid costly mistakes.

"From $500 to Financial Freedom—How Real People Used Dividends to Change Their Lives"

While theory is great, nothing beats **real examples** of how dividend investing works in practice. In this chapter, we profile investors at every stage—from beginners to retirees—showing what works, what fails, and how to grow through experience.

18.1 Real Portfolio Breakdowns

Case Study #1: The "High-Yield Disaster"

Investor Profile: Retiree chasing income
Portfolio:

•50% in ultra-high yield (>8%) – AGNC, ORC, SDIV
•30% in risky REITs – NYMT, TWO
•20% in speculative energy MLPs – MPLX, EPD
Result:

•Dividend cuts wiped out 40% of income in 2020.

•Capital erosion – Portfolio dropped 50%+ in market downturns.
•Forced to sell assets to cover living expenses.
Lesson:
❌ High yield ≠ Safe income. Always check payout sustainability.

Case Study #2: The "Dividend Growth Millionaire"

Investor Profile: Long-term wealth builder
Portfolio:

•40% Dividend Aristocrats – JNJ, PG, KO
•30% Growth Dividend Stocks – AAPL, MSFT, AVGO
•20% REITs (low debt, high quality) – O, WPC
•10% Cash (for buying opportunities)
Result:

•Dividend income grew 10% annually for 15 years.
•Portfolio value doubled despite market crashes.
•Never sold shares—lived off dividends alone.
Lesson:
✅ Quality + Growth = Long-term success.

□ **Susan (Age 66) – Retirement Income Focused**

- Portfolio Size: $850,000
- Dividend Yield: 4.5%
- Monthly Income: ~$3,200
- Strategy: Mix of REITs, Dividend Aristocrats, JEPI, and SCHD

- Key Holdings: O, PG, JNJ, VICI, SCHD, VYM
- Retirement Plan: Reinvest 10% of dividends to offset inflation

📌 *Susan lives mostly off her dividends and hasn't sold a stock in 3 years.*

💰 *18.2 Long-Term Dividend Wealth Stories*

The "Coffee Can Portfolio" Investor

Strategy:

•Bought 10 blue-chip dividend stocks in 1990 (e.g., MCD, PEP, JNJ).
•Never sold, reinvested dividends for 30+ years.
Result:

•100*k*→2.5M+ (with $80k/year in dividends).
•Outperformed the S&P 500 due to compounding.
0

Key Takeaway:
✔ Time + Reinvestment = Unstoppable wealth.

The "Sector Rotation Genius"

Strategy:

•Rotated into beaten-down sectors (e.g., energy in 2020, banks in 2009).
•Bought high-quality dividend payers at lows.

Result:

•Yield on cost >15% on some positions.
•Capital gains + rising dividends = 20%+ annualized returns.
Key Takeaway:
✔ Contrarian investing + dividends = Massive upside.

👨‍💻 Kevin (Age 42) – FIRE (Financial Independence Retire Early)

- Retired at 39 using a $1.3M portfolio
- 80% in dividend stocks/ETFs, 20% in cash & bonds
- Income Strategy: $45K/year in dividends + Roth conversions
- Top Holdings: AVGO, AAPL, SCHD, VYMI, QYLD
- Manages risk via sector balancing and periodic reallocation

📌 *Kevin uses a "yield ladder" to match income to monthly expenses, avoiding sequence-of-returns risk.*

⌛ *18.3 Early Retirement with Dividends*

Case Study: Retired at 45 with Dividends

Investor Profile: Engineer, saved aggressively
Strategy:

•Built a $1.2M portfolio by 45.
•Targeted 4% yield ($48k/year in dividends).

•50% defensive stocks (UTLs, healthcare), 50% growth (Tech, Industrials).

Result:

•Quit job at 45, lived off dividends.
•Dividends grew faster than inflation (5-7% annually).
•Portfolio continued growing despite withdrawals.

Lesson:

✅ You don't need a 10% yield to retire early—just sustainability.

👨💻 Kevin (Age 42) – FIRE (Financial Independence Retire Early)

- Retired at 39 using a $1.3M portfolio
- 80% in dividend stocks/ETFs, 20% in cash & bonds
- Income Strategy: $45K/year in dividends + Roth conversions
- Top Holdings: AVGO, AAPL, SCHD, VYMI, QYLD
- Manages risk via sector balancing and periodic reallocation

📌 *Kevin uses a "yield ladder" to match income to monthly expenses, avoiding sequence-of-returns risk.*

📈 *18.4 Beginner to Expert Journey*

The "From Zero to $1M Dividends" Story

Phase 1 (Beginner – Mistakes):

•Chased penny stock dividends (cut within months).
•Bought overleveraged REITs (wiped out 30% in 2008).
Phase 2 (Learning – Shift to Quality):

•Focused on dividend aristocrats.
•Started tracking payout ratios, debt levels.
Phase 3 (Expert – Optimized Strategy):

•Tax-efficient accounts (held REITs in IRA).
•Sector diversification (no more than 20% in one industry).
•Dividend growth focus (5%+ annual hikes).
Result:

•0→1M portfolio in 12 years.
•$40k/year in dividends (all reinvested).
Lesson:
✔ Every expert was once a beginner—learn from mistakes.

👩 Emma (Age 28) – Started Investing in 2020

- Began with $1,000 in Robinhood
- Bought KO, O, VTI, SCHD
- Discovered DRIPs and started reinvesting every dividend
- Now investing $500/month, portfolio ~ $18,000
- Learning to build a long-term, low-turnover portfolio

□ Insight:

Dividend investing is beginner-friendly and builds confidence. Watching income grow is highly motivating.

💡 *18.5 Dividend Investing Lessons Learned*

The 5 Hardest-Won Lessons from Real Investors

1."High Yield is Usually a Trap" – Most >6% yields cut eventually.
2."Dividend Growth > Starting Yield" – A 2% yielder growing at 10% beats a 6% flat payer.
3."Taxes Matter" – REITs/MLPs in taxable accounts can be brutal.
4."Sector Diversification is Non-Negotiable" – 2008 (banks), 2020 (energy) taught us this.
5."Cash is a Position" – Having dry powder in crashes lets you buy bargains.

Lesson	Explanation
"Slow and steady wins"	Compound growth > market timing or meme stock chasing
"Don't chase yield"	High yield often signals high risk
"Income > net worth in retirement"	Cash flow matters more than account balance
"Reinvest early, harvest later"	DRIP early on, then switch to cash income in retirement
"Tax strategy is everything"	Roth/Traditional IRA mix + tax-efficient ETF placement

🔍 **Bonus Takeaways from Real Investors**

- Track dividend income like a business revenue line
- Build a watchlist and add during corrections—not highighs

- Review portfolio yield + growth rate annually (target 3–5% yield with 5–7% growth)
- Focus on **dividend safety** (low payout ratio, consistent FCF)

🚦 **Bottom Line**

Real people are using dividend investing to retire early, live off passive income, and grow serious long-term wealth. Whether you're starting with $500 or $500,000, **discipline, diversification, and dividend growth** are your ticket to financial freedom.

🎯 *Final Takeaways: How to Build a Bulletproof Dividend Portfolio*

✅ Start Early, Reinvest Dividends – Compounding is your best friend.
✅ Focus on Quality, Not Just Yield – Payout ratio <75%, strong balance sheet.
✅ Diversify Across Sectors – No more than 20% in one industry.
✅ Hold Some Cash – For buying opportunities in crashes.
✅ Learn from Others' Mistakes – Don't repeat the high-yield disasters.

Biggest Mistake to Avoid:
❌ Thinking dividends are "passive income" without research.

By studying these **real-world cases**, you can **avoid pitfalls** and **fast-track your success**.

The Shocking Truth About Dividend Investor Case Studies (What No One Admits)

Most dividend investing stories you hear are survivorship bias at work—only the winners get publicity, while the failures stay hidden. This chapter reveals the uncomfortable realities behind dividend success stories, plus pro tips and hidden traps you won't hear about in mainstream finance circles.

💣 *The Bombshell Reality: "Most Dividend Portfolios FAIL"*

What People Get Wrong:

They assume all dividend investors eventually succeed if they "buy and hold." The truth? Most blow up because of these unspoken mistakes:

1. *The "Yield Illusion" Trap*
   - Example: A retiree puts 100% into AGNC (14% yield) → Dividend gets cut → Portfolio collapses.
   - Why? They ignored payout sustainability (AGNC's dividend wasn't covered by earnings).

2. *The "Sector Concentration Disaster"*

•Example: An investor loaded up on bank stocks in 2007 → 2008 crisis → Dividends suspended.

•Why? No sector diversification.

3. *The "Tax Bomb" Nobody Warned Them About*

•Example: Holding MLPs (like EPD) in a taxable account → Surprise K-1 forms + higher taxes.

•Why? They didn't research tax implications.

Pro-Tip:

✔ Backtest your strategy against 2008, 2020 crashes—would your portfolio survive?

💡 *The "Secret Sauce" of Truly Successful Dividend Investors*

What the Winners Do Differently:

1. *They Focus on Dividend GROWTH, Not Just Yield*

•Example: $10k in AAPL (0.6% yield in 2012) → Now yields 10%+ on cost due to growth.

•Loser Move: Chasing AT&T's 7% yield (which got cut in half).

2. *They Keep a "Crash Shopping List"*

•Example: In March 2020, smart buyers loaded up on O, JNJ, PEP at 30% discounts.

•Loser Move: Panic-selling instead of buying.

3. *They Use Tax-Advantaged Accounts Strategically*

•Example: Holding REITs (like O) in an IRA to avoid taxable income.
•Loser Move: Keeping REITs in a taxable account (higher tax rate).

Pro-Tip:
✔ Track "yield on cost" (not just current yield) to see real progress.

⚠ *Hidden Pitfalls in Dividend Case Studies*

1. The "Backtest Bias" Deception

•Many success stories cherry-pick time periods (e.g., "Look how well my portfolio did since 2009!" – yeah, after the crash).
•Reality: Try the same strategy starting in 2007—many would have failed.
Fix:
✔ Stress-test your portfolio against multiple market cycles.

2. The "Reinvestment Fantasy"

•Stories often assume dividends are always reinvested perfectly—but in reality:
•Brokerages charge fees for DRIP.
•Fractional shares aren't always available.
•Taxes complicate reinvestment in taxable accounts.

Fix:

✔ Use a low-cost broker (like Fidelity) with free fractional shares.

3. The "Invisible Fees" Drain

•Many dividend ETFs (like SDY, VYM) have hidden turnover costs that erode returns.
•Example: A 2% yield minus 1% in fees/taxes = 1% real return.
Fix:
✔ Prefer individual stocks over high-fee ETFs.

🎯 3 Unusual Pro-Tips from Veteran Dividend Investors

1. The "Drip-and-Switch" Strategy

•How it works:

1. Reinvest dividends automatically (DRIP).
2. Once a year, sell overweight positions and rebalance into undervalued stocks.

•Why? Avoids overconcentration risk.

2. The "Dividend Trap Early Warning System"

•Monitor:

- •Debt-to-EBITDA > 4x = Danger zone.
- •Payout ratio > 90% (non-REIT) = Red flag.
- •Insider selling = Often precedes cuts.

3. The "Cash Buffer Hack"

•Keep 6 months of expenses in cash—not just for emergencies, but to buy dips without selling stocks.

The Brutal Truth About Early Retirement with Dividends

What Guru Courses Won't Tell You:

•Most "early retirees" quietly go back to work because:

- •They underestimated healthcare costs.
- •Their portfolio yield was too high (and got cut).
- •They didn't account for inflation.

Realistic Path to Early Retirement:

✔ Target 3-4% yield (not 6%+).
✔ Plan for 3% annual inflation.
✔ Keep side income (consulting, rentals) as a backup.

🎯 Final Checklist for Dividend Success

✅ Avoid >6% yields unless you've stress-tested the company.
✅ Hold 20-30 stocks across sectors (no more than 5% in one stock).
✅ Use DRIP wisely—rebalance annually.
✅ Keep cash for crashes (opportunities come when others panic).

Biggest Myth to Debunk:
❌ "Dividend investing is easy." (It's simple, but not easy—requires discipline.)

By learning from **real failures** (not just success stories), you'll build a **truly bulletproof** dividend portfolio.

Lesson	Explanation
"Slow and steady wins"	Compound growth > market timing or meme stock chasing
"Don't chase yield"	High yield often signals high risk
"Income > net worth in retirement"	Cash flow matters more than account balance
"Reinvest early, harvest later"	DRIP early on, then switch to cash income in retirement
"Tax strategy is everything"	Roth/Traditional IRA mix + tax-efficient ETF placement

🔍 **Bonus Takeaways from Real Investors**

- Track dividend income like a business revenue line
- Build a watchlist and add during corrections—not highs
- Review portfolio yield + growth rate annually (target 3–5% yield with 5–7% growth)
- Focus on **dividend safety** (low payout ratio, consistent FCF)

🚦 **Bottom Line**

Real people are using dividend investing to retire early, live off passive income, and grow serious long-term wealth. Whether you're starting with $500 or $500,000, **discipline,**

diversification, and dividend growth are your ticket to financial freedom.

FAQ

1. What is dividend investing?

Dividend investing focuses on buying stocks that pay regular cash dividends (typically quarterly). Investors aim for both income and long-term growth through reinvestment.

2. Is dividend investing worth it?

✅ Yes, if:

•You want passive income (e.g., for retirement).
•You prefer stable companies over speculative growth stocks.
❌ No, if:
•You need short-term gains.
•You chase ultra-high yields (>6%) without researching sustainability.

3. How to start investing in dividend stocks?

1.Open a brokerage account (Fidelity, Schwab, or Interactive Brokers).
2.*Research stocks with:*

- •5+ years of dividend growth
- •Payout ratio <75% (non-REITs)
- •Strong cash flow (e.g., JNJ, PEP, O)

3.*Reinvest dividends (DRIP) to compound returns.*

4. Is dividend investing a good strategy?

•Pros: Steady income, lower volatility, inflation-beating potential.
•Cons: Underperforms growth stocks in bull markets.

•Best for: Long-term investors focused on income + modest growth.

5. Benefits of dividend stocks?

•Passive income (even in market downturns).
•Compounding via reinvestment.
•Historically outperform non-dividend stocks over time.

6. Risks of high-dividend stocks?

•Dividend cuts (if payout is unsustainable).
•Value traps (stock price falls while yield rises).
•Sector risks (e.g., energy stocks tied to oil prices).

7. Risks of high-dividend ETFs?

•High fees (e.g., SDY charges 0.35% annually).
•Overconcentration in risky sectors (e.g., mortgage REITs).
•Tax inefficiency (vs. holding individual stocks).

8. Tax implications of dividend ETFs?

•Qualified dividends: Taxed at 0–20% (if held >60 days).
•Non-qualified/REIT dividends: Taxed as ordinary income.
•MLP ETFs: K-1 tax forms (complex filings).

9. Best platform for dividend investing?

•Fidelity/Schwab: $0 trades, fractional shares, strong research.
•Interactive Brokers: Best for international dividends.
•M1 Finance: Automated DRIP/rebalancing.

10. What to know before investing?

•Avoid stocks with >90% payout ratios.
•Diversify across sectors (no more than 20% in one).
•Track dividend growth (not just yield).

11. How to invest in high-dividend trusts?

•REITs (O, WPC): Focus on funds from operations (FFO) coverage.
•BDCs (MAIN, ARCC): Check net investment income (NII) coverage.
•MLPs (EPD): Hold in tax-advantaged accounts to avoid K-1 hassle.
Pro Tip: Start with a dividend growth ETF (VIG, DGRO) to reduce risk while learning.

Bottom Line: Dividend investing works, but **sustainability matters more than yield**. Stick to quality, diversify, and reinvest wisely. 🚀

Content

www.ingramcontent.com/pod-product-compliance
Lightning Source LLC
Chambersburg PA
CBHW041955260926
51850CB00021B/3431
9782382268285